The Lemurian Science of Immortality

Almine

Plus : The Saradesi Records
of the Fountain of Youth

Published by Spiritual Journeys LLC

First Edition – April 2013

Copyright 2012

P.O. Box 300
Newport, Oregon 97365

www.spiritualjourneys.com

US toll-free phone: 1-877-552-5646

All rights reserved. No part of this publication may be reproduced without crediting the author as the originator. Parts exceeding one printed page in length may be reproduced only with the written permission of the publishers.

Cover Artwork by Charles Frizzell

Manufactured in the United States of America

ISBN 978-1-936926-20-6 (Softcover)
ISBN 978-1-936926-21-3 (Adobe Reader)

Table of Contents

Endorsements VII

Introduction 1

Book I. The Saradesi Records – The Fountain of Youth

Excerpts From the Saradesi Teachings 8

Concepts of the Saradesi Records Part I *11*

Concepts of the Saradesi Records 13

Erasing the Memory of Aging through Internal Technology 22

Concepts of the Saradesi Records Part II *31*

Excerpts from the Lemurian Records 37

The Round Tablets of Saradesi 46

The Wisdom of the Joints of Man 48

The 144 Tones of the Song of the Joints of Man 61

The Alchemical Equation of The 144 Tones of the Joints 62

The Voice of the Divine Feminine 87

Book II: The Lemurian Tablets of Life and Death – Power Source of the Alchemists

The Forming of Directions (The Epic Tale of Gilhamet) 98

The Frequencies of Adventure 104

The Forming of Life and Death and the Cycles of Existence 140

The 24 Animalistic Natures 145

The Split that Caused the First Nature to Form – from the Writings of the Imlakee Tribe 151

The Urban Jungle 156
Entering the Labyrinth 163
Dissolving the Mazes 169
    Daily Meditation to Access New Potential....................................... 172
Youthfulness and Health from Ancient Lemurian Texts 176
Excerpts from the Lemurian Records 183
    The Meditation for the Restoration of Youth 199
    The Meditation of Renewal... 208
    The Meditation of Youthening 214
The Genitals and the Fountain of Youth 217
    The Meditation of the Fountain of Youth... 218
The Mystical Properties of the Vagina and Penis 222
    Meditation to Restore the Mystical Abilities 222

Bonus Section: The Illuminations of Eternal Life 227

Introduction to the God Kingdom 229
Illuminations of the Gods 237
Closing 385

Endorsements

"What a priceless experience to be able to catch a glimpse into one of the most remarkable lives of our time ..."

> H.E. Ambassador Armen Sarkissian,
> Former Prime Minister of the Republic of Armenia,
> Astrophysicist, Cambridge University, UK

"I'm really impressed with Almine and the integrity of her revelations. My respect for her is immense and I hope that others will find as much value in her teachings as I have."

> Dr. Fred Bell,
> Former NASA Scientist
> Author of *The Promise*

"The information she delivers to humanity is of ihe highest clarity. She is fully deserving of her reputation as the leading mystic of our age."

> Zbigniew Ostas, Ph.D Quantum Medicine,
> Somatidian Orthobiology, Canada and Poland

Introduction

Man has always marveled at the few among them who have managed to overcome the ravages of time: aging and death. Historical records, such as those found in Genesis in the Bible, indicate that at least certain lineages retained their virility and longevity hundreds of years longer than modern man.

As the Earth fell in density, the Pre-Diluvian records containing the secrets of these youthening practices were lost. Only advanced mystics able to travel between realms of different densities were able to access them. Rumors of the immortals in Florida spread to Europe.

In ancient Lemuria, called the Motherland (Ma-ad, in the Lemurian tongue), the Saradesi, Fountain of Youth practices were carried by missionaries (called Naga) to India, China, Ethiopia, Egypt and other countries. A missionary couple called Amaraka and Amaraku carried them to Peru, where the first Peruvian empire was established.

Further sets of records were carried by the missionary couple called Iy and Taya during Atlantis'[1] third period. During this time Atlantis consisted of two large islands called Itaya and Ruta. A few pockets of practitioners of the ancient rejuvenation secrets survived in the area of what became Florida and the Yucatan, Mexico, after the sinking of Atlantis.

---

1   See *Secrets of the Hidden Realms*.

PONCE DE LEON AND THE FOUNTAIN OF YOUTH

The Fountain of Youth is a legendary spring supposed to reverse aging and bestow perpetual youth on those who drink of its waters. Accounts of this mythical, magical water have circulated for several thousand years, appearing in writing by Herodotus and in stories about Prester John. Its supposed location has varied with the teller. Stories of similar waters were also prevalent throughout much of the Caribbean during the Age of Exploration, including accounts of water with restorative powers in the mythical land of Bimini.

The legend is most popularly associated with the Spanish explorer Juan Ponce de Leon, who allegedly embarked on a mission to find the restorative spring. His travels took him to what is now Florida in 1513 where it is said he ended his search at or near what is now the city of St. Augustine. Early in the 20th century, enterprising promoters capitalized on the legend and incorporated it into campaigns to lure vacationers to the area.

St. Augustine continues to be widely advertised as the presumptive location of the Fountain of Youth.

Excerpt, Wikipedia

THE RESTORATION OF THE SECRETS OF REJUVENATION

The ability of Almine to restore the ancient secrets of overcoming aging, death and decay is a miraculous gift to humankind. Her extraordinary gifts of being able to translate ancient lost languages and to travel into and retrieve information from etheric realms have produced this remarkable book.

Previous Records Translated by Almine
Photographed Interdimensionally

Photos by Barbara Rotzoll, 2009 (angelbarbara.com)

The same records were drawn several months before their interdimensional photo was taken

Image drawn by Eva, Canada

Book I

The Saradesi Records

THE FOUNTAIN OF YOUTH

If the female had not separated from the male, she would not afterward have died with the male. His separation was the inception of death ...

Excerpt from the Gospel of Philip, one of the Gnostic Gospels, a text of the New Testament Apocrypha, dating back to approximately the 3rd century and rediscovered in a cave near Nag Hammadi in 1945.

Excerpts From the Saradesi Teachings

A VISIT FROM A LEMURIAN MASTER

"As I was doing Almine's hair, I looked through the window and saw a female being in the back seat of her car. The being then came into the salon and told me her name was Tri-ech-ma.

She was quite impatient with me as I struggled with her strange language. She relayed information to Almine who wrote it down. When she left, she said good-bye to me with the words: 'Avanach-edna-eesh', which Almine translated as, 'until we meet again.'"

Roxanne, Hairdresser
Newport, Oregon

TRI-ECH-MA'S MESSAGE

Skabavich velechstra hurunit plavak arestranech huresta bruvabek.

Within you, the fountain of Living Waters waits to come forth and renew your body.

The inner resources cannot be accessed when you are more familiar with the outer than the inner realities. Eternal renewal comes when the inner and outer realities are one. The five senses communicate with the 'outer' realities. The 'inner' realities use the inner senses.

TRI-ECH-MA ANSWERS QUESTIONS

Q. When my hairdresser put Aragan oil on my hair, you said it was part of the information ... is it Argan oil? I thought you said Aragan?
A. It is known by those that use it now as Argan, but called by those who planted the trees in Morocco long ago as Araga-an or Aragan.

Q. Which means 'giver of heavenly light ...'
A. Yes, because of its properties.

Q. But who planted them?
A. Some who came to Earth from Nibiru – a distant system that comes into this solar system every few thousand years ...

Q. Were the trees from there as well?
A. No, they grew in other areas in Northern Africa. They were found to reset the memory of the skin. Old skin would forget that it is 'old' and behave as young skin would ...

Q. Is it 100% effective, and are there other products that do the same?
A. Only a powerful practitioner of 'inner' technology can be 100% effective, but there are products that help: a mushroom that looks like a bishop's hat found in Ethiopia; also rhodium and iridium help. Therefore, pure aloe vera gel on the skin and taken internally does as well – it is rich in rhodium and iridium.

Q. What is this freshwater plant that you are showing me?
A. The ancients call it Minachve. It grew in water, rich in trace elements. It is very powerful in erasing memories of age in the body. It can be taken internally, or its gel can be used topically.

Q. But where can one find it?
A. It is rare. There is some in Borneo, in water-filled sink-holes in the mountains.

Concepts of the Saradesi Records

PART I

Speak now in silence ...
In wordless thunder roar

Concepts of the Saradesi Records

Unlike many of the ancient records, the section of the Saradesi records known as 'Menechsta' which means the 'The Unveiling', does not speak only to the mind, but to the heart as well.

The language is poetic in its deliverance of the concepts. By using poetry, it leads one to ponder its multi-layered meaning rather than accept it at face value.

The poetic perspective allows omnisensory perception to develop. It is an experience that involves the whole body and all senses to feel the meaning behind the words. It is in the non-cognitive feeling of these concepts that the journey into a deathless existence begins ...

Note: When reading the excerpts from the Saradesi Records on the following pages, it is important to understand that there are multiple meanings the lie beneath the words. They must be felt, rather than taken at face value.

The Known and the Unknown

I taste the foreign air upon my tongue – alien in its newness …

It entices me to forsake the cushioned paltriness of the known

To follow the song of the beckoning unknowable spontaneously, according to ancient patterns of joy.

Almine's Note
In familiarity lies stagnation and decay, if it is embraced as the desirable status alone. The phrase, 'according to ancient patterns of joy,' which is experienced as the known, suggests that the known, unknown and unknowable should be embraced to produce constant rejuvenation.

The Depth of Seeking a Home

Wrestling like the wind harassing the trees,
I conjure the concept of home
Then follow the myth across the edge of dawn
With dogged determination to make it real …

Ku-arch harsut arch-parvaa unas bruharset staruvaa
Subach-tu nanasut heresh asta uvechva herestu

Almine's Note
This concept suggests that beyond the horizon of our sensory perceptions lies the more feminine realities that give us roots and make us feel at home. The wind, like the mind, has no roots – only wings, which is a masculine quality. It is unanchored and thus seeks to anchor itself by opposing (wrestling with) the trees. Inner conflict is the single greatest cause of aging. This passage gives the cause of opposition: it is created by mind to anchor itself.

The Black Moon

Beyond the horizon, what shall I see
but the black moon beckoning me …
What is taken, what is lost
artificiality becomes replaced
So it was when the black moon left
beyond the horizon of mind …

Almine's Note
A splitting of realities had taken place when duality formed: a black light reality containing the black moon (feminine) and a white light reality that we are living in (masculine). The gaps this left in each reality became filled with artificial life. The masculine reality we are living in felt homeless since the feminine part that left produces the self-nurtured (at-home) feeling. The feminine components of this reality are a secondary creation, like scar tissue on a wound.

Interdimensional Photos of the White Moon and the Black Moon

Note the smaller moon entering the picture on the bottom right (above) and then moving in front of the other moon (below)

The two moons from separate realities were seen simultaneously in February 2010.

Photos taken by Shelley, Canada, during Almine's Retreat in Tampa.

The Missing Component of the Human Heart

With the high heart in the sternum,
the black moon was one
Thus an artificial ghost of the high heart,
like a turquoise shadow lingers on …
The high heart fled with the black moon
The heart and the white moon
cried for their feminine counterparts …

Almine's Note
Whatever happens in the macrocosm happens in man – the cosmic archetype. When realities split, man inhabited both realities. In the black light reality, the heart of man is in the sternum as a turquoise chakra. Separated, each heart, like the moons, yearns for its lost counterpart. Native Americans wear turquoise on their sternums to restore the frequency that has been lost.

Questioning the Purpose of Duality

Aging comes when leakages of resources
cry out their emptiness
The wolf howls for the real moon to return ...
What is given away?
What is lost?
What wisdom has been bought at such a cost?
Speak now from the land of black rivers ...
I call through the veil of silver mist ...

*Kaanigvit hurasta pilak nestu vilavech
sparurat minush hurat varset herestu*

Almine's Note
Life becomes cyclical – cycles of death (living in the black light reality) and life (living in the white light reality). This excerpt calls across the division of these realities for answers to reveal themselves as to what has been gained by this separation.

The Source of the Tyranny of Form

The answer came: The sun holds you captive

in a world of form

Above your head Arelu holds the reign

from the day you were born

The high heart shape-shifts

Like a phantom goddess between the veils of time

No bane is space when you dance with time …

Almine's Note
Arelu means 'the little sun.' This refers to the Lahun or tenth chakra, depicted in Egyptian or Sumerian art as a golden disc above the head. The illusion of space was never meant to become a 'reality', but rather to be like lines drawn in the sand through which the high heart enables us to spontaneously dance. The movements of creation have gone around and around in the circle of spaces created by mind. The high heart, once restored, enables us to dance through time in any direction we choose, replacing programs with artistry.

The Conspiracy of Heart and Mind

Entwined in conspiracy, the heart and the mind
The heart sustaining the mental games to control
The high heart lies like the black moon, unseen
It is the most feminine, heavenly queen
Sovereign in expression – a worthy counterpart …

Almine's Note
The masculine reality's feminine counterpart supports the tyranny of mind. The heart panders to the mind while the mind creates opposition for the heart, or feminine, while ensnaring it in its rules and categories and division. With the restoration of the feminine part of the heart, sovereign feminine expression is restored.

Erasing the Memory of Aging through Internal Technology

The body forms as scar tissue from the splitting of the psyche.

It is thus a 'shadow,' which is the result of two poles pulling apart.

The more we fight against shadows, the more it erodes our own body.

The following mystical technique can only be done by understanding the nature of shadows.

What is form but light defined by shadows? Would we else not seem as a candle inside the sun — undifferentiated from one another? Bless then the shadows of existence, for without them you would not be able to play the game of life.

Excerpt from the Saradesi Tablets

THE NATURE OF SHADOWS

Shadows are inextricably woven together with opposite poles; one cannot exist without the other. If a wound separates the skin, a space forms. If scar tissue does not fill the gap, resources leak out – in the case of the skin, blood is spilled. To deny that the new scar tissue is part of your knee, nose or other injured part because it subsequently formed as a reaction is as unreasonable as denying the right of our shadow to exist.

For eons we have fought against shadows and the beings that represent them. One strengthens that which one opposes. The rigid programs of our bodies, societies and other patterns are due to the strengthening of scarring.

The body is the 'scar tissue' of the psyche's splitting. It is then a 'shadow' and the more we fight against shadows, the more it erodes our own body. Youthening happens when we embrace our shadows. Without them the game of life cannot be played within existence.

Most bodies have some form of inflammation. A self-war has been waged within us and within the cosmos. The masculine has thought of the feminine as incapable of guiding life, not realizing it was not the real feminine. The masculine and feminine both have thought of shadow as being unworthy of life.

First Method to Erase the Memory of Aging

Place yourself in a deeply relaxed state. Breathe deeply until all tension is gone.

Realization 1

The masculine, feminine and shadow components of yourself are the mind, heart's emotions and the body. If the body does not exist neither can the mind or emotions express. The body holds them together.

Visualization 1

Imagine an ocean of luminous, gentle tones. The ocean has no end and has always existed. Within its colors flowing through one another, a sphere is formed and from the resources contained within, individuated forms manifest. The ball is luminous and glowing like the never-ending ocean but each time something is formed, resources are used.

The ball grows less and less luminous. A tear forms in the membrane that separates the ball from the ocean. To keep the ball as a separate area to play and explore in, scar tissue quickly forms to fill the gap.

The membrane is designed to insulate the ball from the ocean; the scar tissue is a type of bridge and can draw new resources from the ocean into the ball. Our bodies can draw resources from the vastness of Infinite Being into our lives.

Realization 2

The body is at the cutting edge where Creation meets Creator. It has the ability to erase past memories of how life 'used to be' and also to release the rigidity that forms as a result of defending its right to exist. Many seek erroneously to transcend the body, but the body is the needed foundation for individuated life.

Visualization 2

The fact that you exist as an individuated being means that you also have a shadow self and a black light/frequency self in a parallel reality. See this body stand in radiant white light in the middle of the starry sky. Hold this vision until you can really start to see it. See yourself become one with this white light body. Close your eyes (in your vision) and sense the presence of your black light self through a door in space in a parallel reality. Open that door with intent. Through another door, see all your selves. Draw a deep breath in and as you do so, see your other selves join as one with this one. As they do, force your breath out, see your combined selves explode into a white light sun, while simultaneously exploding into the frequency of grateful acknowledgement of the perfection of existence.

Draw in another deep breath and this time force it out as light and grateful acknowledgement of the perfection. Feel the lightness and contentment of the body at peace as the breath is released.

You may repeat this exercise with the breathe as many times as you wish.

ALMINE ANSWERS STUDENTS' QUESTIONS

Q. What does Saradesi mean exactly?
A. 'The Gates of Youth.'

Q. It is not a Lemurian word. What language is it?
A. The ancient language of the Embodiment of the Infinite spoken during the descension cycles when life entered the black light reality.

Q. What does it mean to speak through one's hair? This was mentioned through the Song of the Wild Dog's communication.
A. Bodily hair assists in erasing old patterns that cause aging and by communicating the Song of Life that is always new, for you to interpret.

Q. What does the flash of light accomplish in the technique of combining all three bodies together?
A. It erases the memory held by the feminine, black light component.

Q. And the surge of grateful acknowledgment of the perfection?
A. It dissolves the masculine, white lights partitions, divisions and belief systems. The body is both magnetic and electric and benefits from both these steps.

Second Method to Erase the Memory of Aging

When illusion is kept in the memories of our body, it begs for release. It speaks to us through the Poetry of Dreaming and dream symbols (these methods are described in the book *Labyrinth of the Moon*), and other methods.

Unresolved illusions that have not yielded their insights hold memories of aging in the body and are areas from which resources are leaked. This causes aging and physical decay.

Automatic drawing of symbols is one method of allowing these old memories to speak to you. Jaylene, Almine's 12-year-old daughter, demonstrated this method of releasing and erasing these old memories of aging:

1. Empty the mind through meditation, or by entering into timelessness by experiencing pure beingness the way a child would.

2. Secondly, allow yourself to draw anything that comes to you without engaging the mind.

3. Afterwards, analyze or read the story that the images collectively tell.

EXAMPLE DRAWN BY JAYLENE, 12 YEARS OLD

EXPLANATION[2] OF THE ILLUSTRATION

1. The diamond or gemstone indicates something of value.
2. The swastika is the symbol for artificial life.
3. The box with gemstones or treasure indicates value that is hidden. A box is the symbol for belief systems so this symbol could mean: belief systems are obscuring value.
4. The circle with the equilateral cross is a symbol used by Native Americans to indicate the 4 directions. Jaylene is Native American.

---

[2] See *Labyrinth of the Moon*, by Almine for detailed information on how to interpret symbols.

PUTTING THE MESSAGE TOGETHER

The value of artificial life (grids and matrices that form from programs and belief systems) is overlooked because of our belief systems (we believe it to be less real than the rest of life, for instance). It has been valuable (the gem) in creating directional space for individuation and Creation to take place.

Concepts of the Saradesi Records

PART II

Man crucifies himself with unmet expectations.
Because he is the Cosmic Archetype,
he thereby crucifies all.

Almine

The Demise of Frequency

Speak now in silence. In wordless thunder roar ...
No more strife held in the voice
Nor more intent to persuade and be heard ...
Nor desire to be understood,
for from desire limitation is born
In desiring something,
lack is created and deficiency emphasized

Almine's Note
Communication needs to take place from the vastness of Self – not through the voice of the little self wanting to be heard. The agenda of the little self wanting to be understood cuts us off from limitless supply because it needs something from the 'external'. This limitation causes aging. If we live in the knowing of ourselves as all things, communication is enhanced by coming from the greater Self. It is ourself speaking to ourself without agenda.

Balancing Imbalance

Imbalance persists, no matter how many times we try to make it go away – imbalance will not die

Linear change is cyclical and always repeats itself, though higher each time

To transcend the illusion that around in a circle goes

Balance first the opposites, then unite them as one

In joining balanced opposites, they cancel each other and both are gone.

Almine's Note
Transformation, transmutation and transfiguration are the three stages of linear change. Because they go around in a circle, nothing really changes and all repeats itself. To be free from the wheel's turning, transcend by moving above it. This is done by balancing opposites and joining them as one, releasing the illusions that bind one to a lower reality. The balancing of opposites can be accomplished by valuing both equally – living without value judgements.

The Origin of the Linear Stages of Change

The triad of change – three sisters are they
Whence did the stages of linear change originate
From three illusions are they born
all having the same cause ...
Transformation comes from the desire for beauty
Transmutation from the desire for abundance
Transfiguration comes from wanting power
All three are rooted in increase's cause
Always hungry, always wanting more

Almine's Note
The three linear stages of change are the result of perceived lack. The desire for increase forms separation and causes change to separate into these stages. These linear stages lie on a two-dimensional plane – like a horizontal turning wheel. The horizontal plane is feminine (hence they are called sisters) and they represent the directions of above, below and within.

Inter-dimensional Nutrients

Chromium, Phosphorous and Selenium cancel the mirrors of life

Through linear change, we experience

the backwards reflection of mirrors

moving around us like a spinning wheel

When life is externally reflected,

opposition waits upon our way

Reflective nutrients form an inner mirror

Living between two mirrors, we see eternity ...

Almine's Note
The nutrients mentioned are known as reflective. They offset the reversed reflection of our environment. The environment is like a mirror. It reflects a distorted, backwards image, thereby showing us what we are not. The nutrients allow us the self-perception of what we are. These are opposite poles that must be brought into balance so that they can be unified, cancelling one another out. This will eliminate the need to define and attempt to know ourselves. Rhodium and Iridium assist in renewing self-perception by 're-setting' our self-knowledge in the moment.

The Mirror is Created

What is this mirrored wheel

that turns around like a reflective screen

Formed from the sub-atomic building blocks of life[3]

Of seven different frequencies are they made

From them the grids of life, like a wheel are born

Where then do the particles come from

Emitted by his navel, man forms that which keeps all life captive

From his core, little known by most, are they produced

Ensnaring all in a two-dimensional grid

Almine's Note
Man has been called the microcosm of the macrocosm, the archetype of other life forms. There is something as yet unknown about his core that produces the electro-magnetic particles that ensnare all creatures in a two-dimensional wheel of life.

3   See *Windows into Eternity*.

Excerpts from the Lemurian Records

The confident play with geometry

Excerpt 1

I see with my voice. I hear with my vocal chords. Three realities there are: the three sisters are they called – the most masculine one we are. The masculine outputs, the feminine receives. Thus, 'speaking' in our reality is the most developed; it is pro-active. Hearing and seeing are receptive and are most dominant in the other realities. Blind and deaf are the sons and daughters of man until they hear and see through their silences of the voice.

Note: The more feminine realities are denied their voice and self-determination, which comes though the voice. Their only way of expressing has been to be destructive and to hinder the more masculine reality we are in. They have a strong similarity to the three witches of mythology that had only one eye among the three.

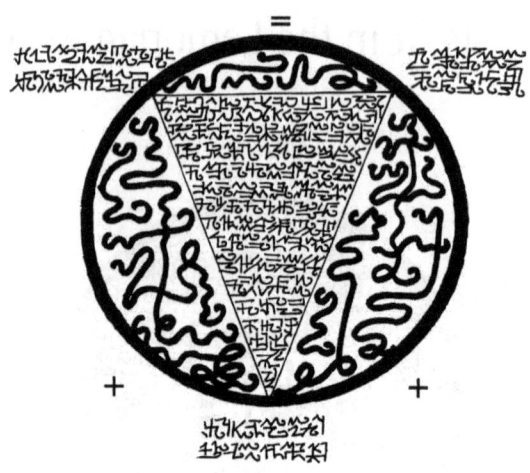

*Confident surfing
of the movement of time*

Excerpt 2

Three moons there are, not two – purple, gold and silver. The only moon we see with lying eyes is the gold one. This is the color of our reality. Three points triangulated produces a reality, thus it has been for life on Earth. But the strongest moon for us has been the gold one. The color yellow or gold holds the alchemical potencies of stability and constancy. Life on Earth has therefore changed its paradigms very slowly.

Note: Living in gold light means that we are more cerebral, logic oriented and more pro-active. The schism of life precludes the ability to live in Oneness because man is the microcosm of the macrocosm. The resources of parts are limited and cannot access unlimited supply through its boundaries.

The appreciation of all levels of consciousness as being a variety of perspectives

Excerpt 3

Three are the goddesses that rule cosmic life. The goddesses of the purple and silver moon made a pact against the goddess of the golden moon, for they resented the voice of the golden goddess dictating the way life should proceed. The Cosmic reality is the joint result of the triangulation of the goddesses. Two thirds of the cosmos is hostile to life on Earth. But they reside on two different planes.

Note: The nature of the cosmos being split into three poles, positive (gold), negative (purple) and silver (neutral) makes living in Oneness difficult. As the microcosm, this schism is reflected as gender in all creatures. The true nature of Oneness, the ultimate goal of mastery, is androgyny. The occurrence of gender is an aberrant phenomenon, the result of an injury. Much of what we take for granted was not always so – something Lemurian and Greek mythology reminds us of.

Knowing relationship to be an alchemical equation of infinite possibilities

Excerpt 4

The pranic tube, the core of man, is artificially created as part of the hostile plans to incarcerate the golden goddess. The silver and purple goddesses implanted the pranic tubes in the golden goddess: a tube that goes from the navel to the ground and as far up. This created the directions of above and below. The same sized tubes go through the navel from front to back and one from side to side. This formed the seven directions that encased the golden goddess and her cosmos, limiting her influence. The colors of the pranic tubes were gold (the vertical one), silver (front to back) and purple (side to side). It is the same for man.

Note: The experience however is blissful and expansive. White light surrounds the body and a violet flame is visible on the head (like the description in the Bible during Pentecost when flames appeared upon the heads of those present). A sphere of light (which is golden) had appeared above my head approximately the size of a large salad plate.[4]

---

4   Excerpt from *Journey to the Heart of God*.

*The undefinable experience of a life
of no opposites*

Excerpt 5

The combined colors of the pranic tubes make a spinning cosmic mirror. The more the golden goddess sees herself in the mirror, the more rigid life in the golden cosmos becomes, for none can define the form of the goddess by gazing upon it without turning to stone; not even the goddess herself. The more life is resisted, the faster the mirrors spin. This uses much energy and resources drain.

Note: Yet again the connection with Greek mythology can be seen as the similarity of the Medusa surfaces. Mythology, the stories that remind us of the forgotten origins of individuated life, began in the Motherland (Lemuria) and went with the Rhamouhal race to Atlantis and from there spread to Europe. The one third of cosmic life we represent fell into density, becoming more and more rigid (turning to stone).

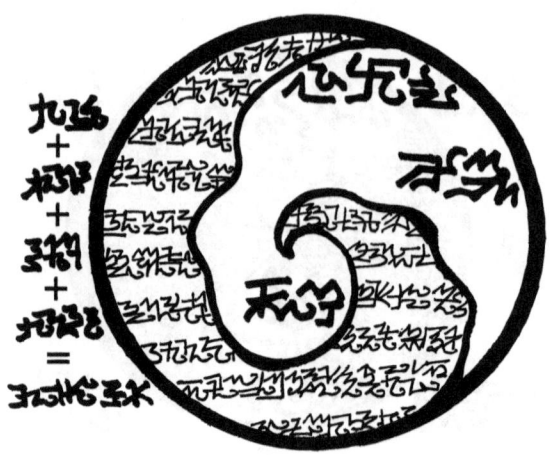

*The Song of the Self as the Undefinable Contradiction.
The harmonious interaction between order and chaos
for an unbounded existence*

Excerpt 6

Where are the memories of that which was done? Why are such momentous cosmic deeds known by none? Memories are erased by design; by the purple and silver goddesses designed. Around each pranic tube lie entwined tendrils like coils that produce an electric current. They wipe clean the memory held in the magnetic components of the pranic tube. The pranic tube is an electro-magnet that is turned into a device that produces an excess of electricity.

Note: Like a Tesla coil, electricity flows between the ends of the Ida and Pingala. The electrical current flows across the top of the brain lobes called by the Lemurian records 'Karanos', which sounds like the Greek 'Kronos'. It is in the Karanos where the primordial memories are kept. It is this area where the electrical current passes through the brain, erasing memories.

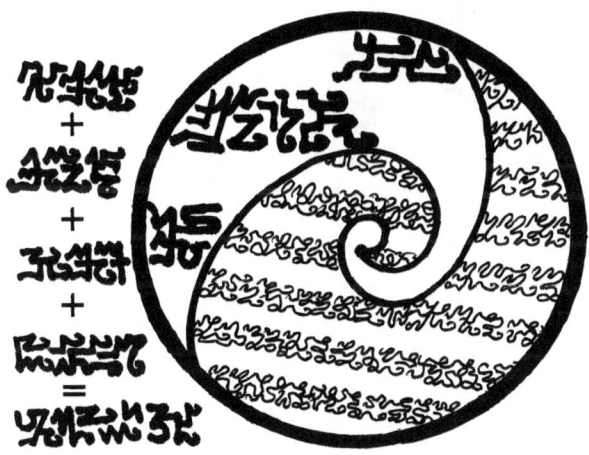

*The Perception of Omni-Perspectives –
the Observer and the Observed Become One.
Living in the unimaginable contradiction of no opposites*

Excerpt 7

Now the pranic tubes must go and the tendrils that around them flow. The cage they made is illusory, step out and set yourself free. Within the base of the spine lies the key. When this information is understood, a crossroads will be reached where many ghosts have stood. No more demise of cosmic parts, no more loss of human capabilities. Let the gold fire consume the pranic tubes and the tendrils around them.

The Technique to Eliminate the Illusion of Pranic Tubes

1. Place yourself in a meditative state.
2. Picture the life-force center behind the navel as a silver ball of light the size of a grapefruit.
3. With the in-breath, envision purple fire being drawn down from the pituitary gland into the life-force center and the gold fire being drawn up from the base of the spine into the life-force center.
4. With each breath the life-force center grows larger.
5. Allow it to build and ignite after many breaths, consuming all pranic tubes and coils until they have disappeared.

Eliminating the Illusion of the Pranic Tube
(This eliminates all 3 pranic tubes)

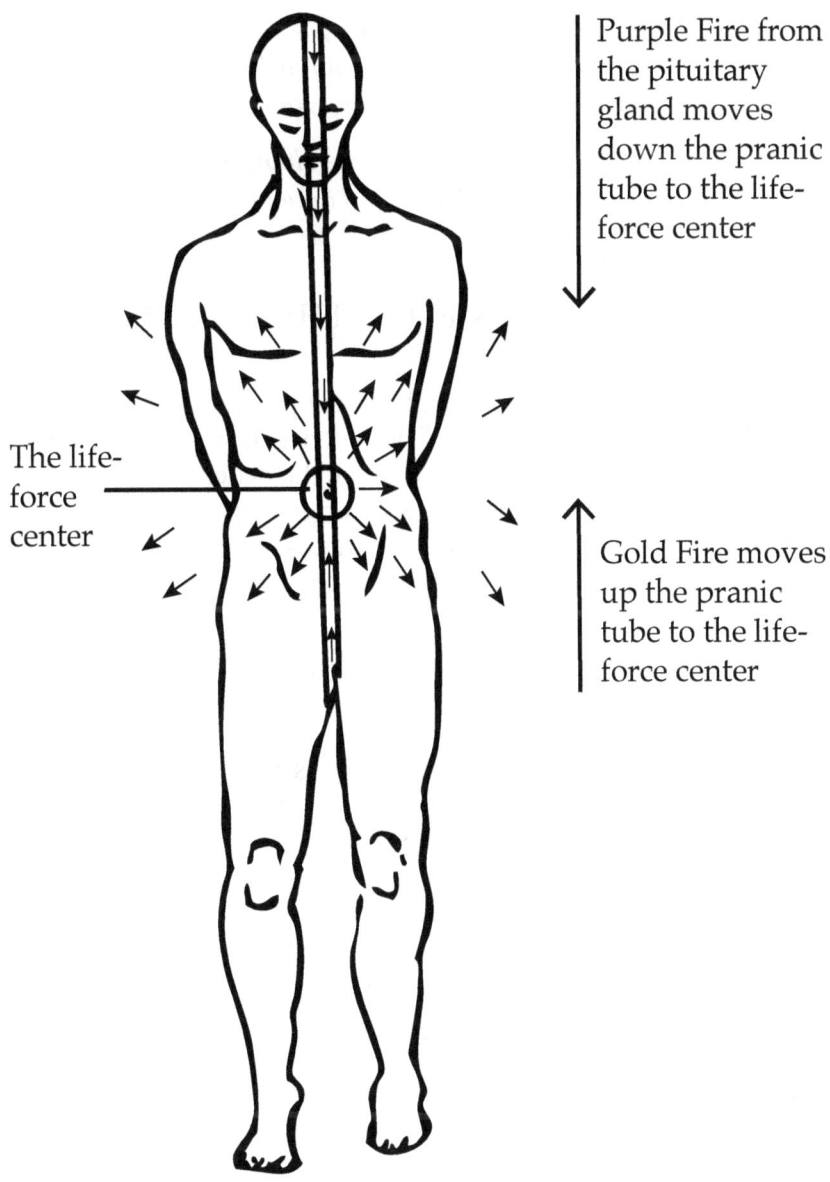

The Round Tablets of Saradesi

*If you seek larger and larger villains,
you shall certainly find them,
for life is a pattern that repeats itself.*

*The pattern can only be changed
from the Oneness of Source.*

TRANSLATION FROM THE TABLETS

Man has hung upon the crucifix of the pranic tubes, crucifying himself by trying to resist life. The patterns continue ever larger, thus what is opposed never ends. Change the pattern by living from Oneness, which creates through you an original cause. Live from the fullness of knowing yourself to be all things, and knowing yourself as the first cause. In a surrendered life, the One moves through you.

INTRODUCTION

The Round Tablets give ways to dissolve self-opposition, the reason most beings on Earth have some form of physical inflammation. The Round Tablets speak of the self as the Portal of Life – a portal that opens through surrender. The loss of resources that cause aging and decay can be reclaimed when the illusion of opposites becomes less real.

The absolute authenticity of expression ensures that Oneness expresses through us. In Oneness, there is nothing to oppose, for there are no opposites.

When we oppose life by clinging to illusions, it effects the joints of the body, making them inflexible. This obscures the insights found in the joints of man.

In the Joints of Man, Great Wisdom Lies
(The numbers indicate where each wisdom is located)

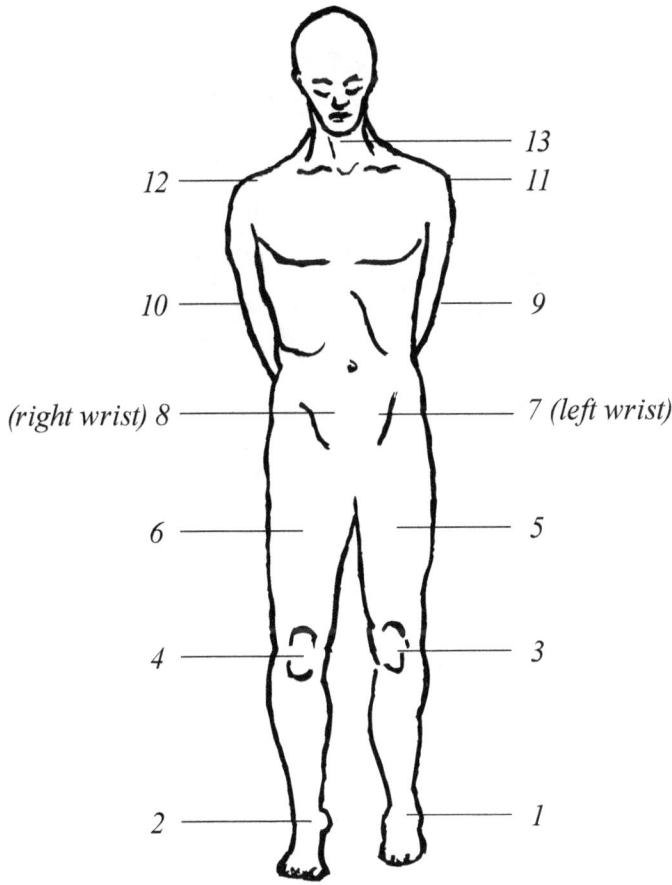

The Wisdom of the Joints of Man

Thirteen joints in the body of man, great wisdom hold
Keys to the alchemy of transcendence that increases manifold
Feel the layers of meaning behind the wisdom's words
They hold thirteen keys to transcend the old, for the new to birth
Ancient the wisdom of the Source of life
Their deeper meaning you must feel inside

The Wisdom of the Joints of Man

Round Tablet 1

Kalach netvi baharus erst uklechvi.
Aranas vibrash minavechvi selevi.

There is neither silence nor movement, but silence observing the movement within itself.

The Lemurian Science of Immortality

Round Tablet 2

*Knuhavach mishavat arech bihastra uhavech
minavish ublechpavi bravabit arestu aharanas.
Knivahur parat eresta uhunuch.*

Wherever the neutral, feminine and masculine become one, separation is transcended. Only then can the currents of life be prodded into a new direction.

Round Tablet 3

Vuhurusba eknech haru-eshvavit haruklas.
Minech satruvi veraspa unas eklet paharusta
velevech.

Life cannot be imagined without polarity, it must be experienced without defining it. Creation was fashioned within duality.

The Lemurian Science of Immortality

Round Tablet 4

Harunach mishevi vrahubastra kni-vechvavi
misha-uhunat klahuva. Sparut stelebi
mira-uset kelsh-vrivesbi.

He who knows change to be the moment's gift and the moment to be the portal into infinity, has transcended linearity.

Round Tablet 5

Minach brivavet ishel avech mirastu herenesvi
arvastu vlivabech arek-va mishelnes
pahur arestak vavi.

The portal of the miraculous life opens when the senses blend into one and the magical body of man yields its secrets.

The Lemurian Science of Immortality

Round Tablet 6

Ku-uhu shuvavesta minavech vi-brash aravesta iharanestu iklech braverevis arveskla pla-uhanet krives pla-uha.

To live without directions in spacelessness requires the complete surrender of a child discovering life with trust for the first time.

Round Tablet 7

Vivabrech miserus vavi prihas kla-unach uvarasbi klave.
Viserut skavet miset uranech plivarus aranas
pra-uhuveret minavives.

Life in linearity has relationships that form the basis of alchemical equations. Transcendant alchemy brings the three poles of life into oneness and always equates to one.

Round Tablet 8

*Kisharat araklas viberat minach uste-vu aklas
biharastat minuch heresta-viskret alachvi miserat
biheresti virsat arklech misheru pribarusvi ikret.*

Beyond the illusion of separatism, lies the indescribable Oneness of life. Transcendental alchemy reduces the oneness of polarity to that which lies beyond the illusion of individuation: the Infinite. It always equates to zero.

Round Tablet 9

Mishavech harestu arek brava viserut akla vrivavet minech ares pelevis astrava mistruch vereva.

Give up now the expectations of what was. When illusion is relinquished, great resources, that will lift you up and over the boundaries of existence, will be yours.

The Lemurian Science of Immortality

Round Tablet 10

Irchva biret, niset arestu. Harak ubavechvi rasta birarut arek pla-uha virska bruvavesbi arunak.

Nothing to change, nothing to understand. Just swim with the currents that in Oneness you may direct.

Round Tablet 11

Kiravesh uhuru nusve klahuvat aresvi prahunak braspech uhunusve bravet eklat prahut berespi kra-unak.
Mishet va-arus prahut aranet pla-una.

Two crutches there are, perception and emotion, on which humanity haltingly walks around and around the cage of his belief systems. Secure in his cage, he fears the unfamiliar wonder without.

Round Tablet 12

*Brivabek asvi mirach anes privat blavelechspi
kranut haresta pla-uha manesh hustava.*

Beyond light and sound, the indescribable awaits where form yields to the intent of a nudge from Oneness.

Round Tablet 13

Akrach unet harasta stubechvi minas kruhanas bi-ustat blihaves unasve minuchvat privek halevespi.

In an ocean of divine compassion I endlessly frolic, renewed in each moment by Divine Intent.

The 144 Tones of the Song of the Joints of Man

Each joint contains three tones that, when combined, form Oneness.

When all 144 tones of the joints are added together, the frequency of immortality is in the body.

THE SONG OF THE JOINTS OF MAN

Transcendent Alchemy, when the full alchemical potencies of sound are present in the joints, creates the frequency of Oneness in the body. This is the first step to eliminating frequency altogether and entering into formless form through Transcendental Alchemy.

Transcendent Alchemy heals duality, bringing about a life of no opposites. Transcendental Alchemy takes us beyond the life of the little self into the merging of the One. Transcendent Alchemy always equals '1,' and Transcendental Alchemy always equals '0.'

A life of no opposites is a life of embracing the contradiction. For the body to relinquish the aging factor of duality, each joint must sing its allotted tones of the One Life. Each of the first twelve joints has 9 frequencies. The 13th joint has 36, totaling 144 tones. When combined together, the 144 tones produce an alchemical equation within man that transcends mortality. In the Lemurian records of Saradesi, it speaks of the body 'Dancing with the Contradiction':

Ekenech harash Vasuva.

The Alchemical Equation of The 144 Tones of the Joints

1. Sleeping in full wakefulness

\+

2. Motionless movement of timelessness

\+

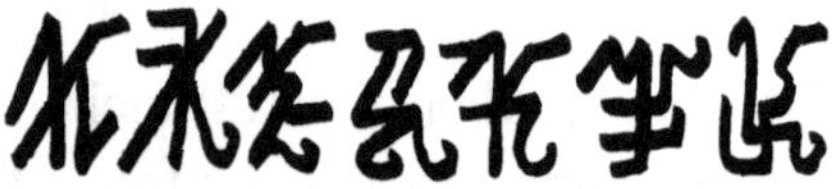

3. Embracing the fullness through emptiness

\+

4. Ageless newness

\+

5. The motionless dance of paradoxes

\+

6. Creating that which has always been

\+

7. Freedom from unimagined boundlessness

\+

8. The thundering voice of silence

\+

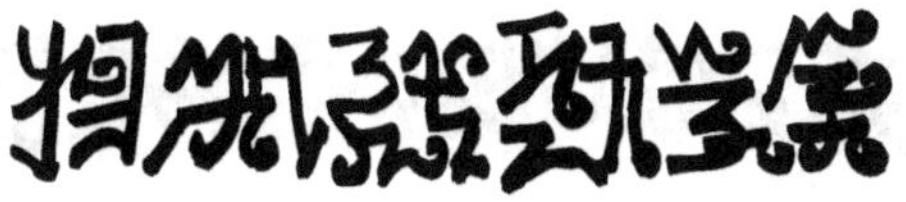

9. Silence watching the movement within itself

\+

10. Finding the without, within

\+

11. Finding oneself at the end of each journey

\+

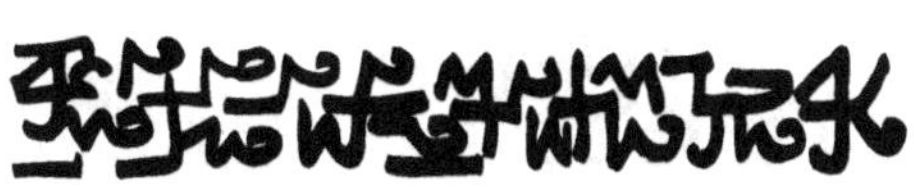

12. Perfection blended into imperfection

\+

Book I. The Saradesi Records — The Fountain of Youth

13. Journey without destination

\+

14. Fluid responsiveness of Eternal Beingness

\+

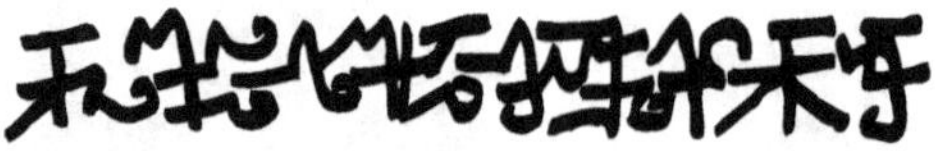

15. Substanceless existence

\+

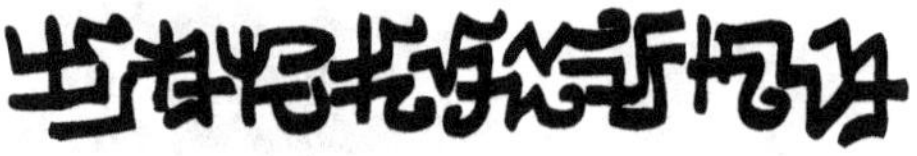

16. Relationshipless interaction

\+

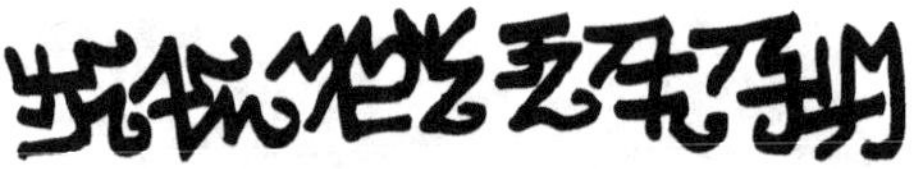

17. Ancient newness of the circle of life

\+

18. The discovery of the known

\+

19. The spontaneous unpredictability of the Divine Plan

\+

20. The complete order of eternal renewal

\+

21. Birthless and deathless continual self-regeneration

\+

22. Undefinable realities

\+

23. Contributing to the quality by not interfering

\+

24. Acknowledging the unrealness of the little self

\+

Book I. The Saradesi Records — The Fountain of Youth

25. The non-differentiation of the One and the many

+

26. The unknowable as Self

+

27. The imagined dream of form

+

28. The interchangeable senses

+

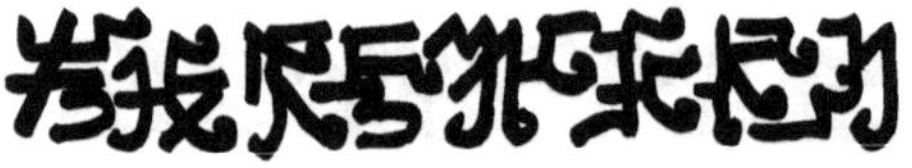

29. Removing illusion by dynamic balance

+

30. Resolving duality by disacknowledging it

+

31. Removing the need for illusion by seeing its purpose

+

32. Finding what was never lost

+

33. Acknowledging not knowing as the greatest wisdom

+

34. Combining expansion and contraction into one

+

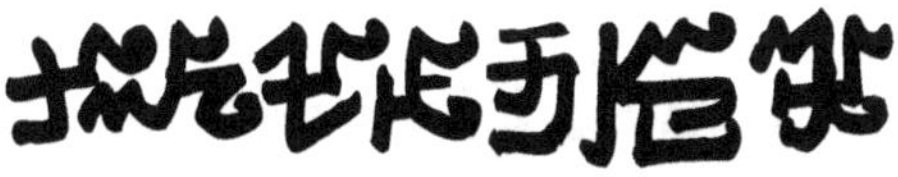

35. Directionless guidance

+

36. Moving beyond boundaries that never were

+

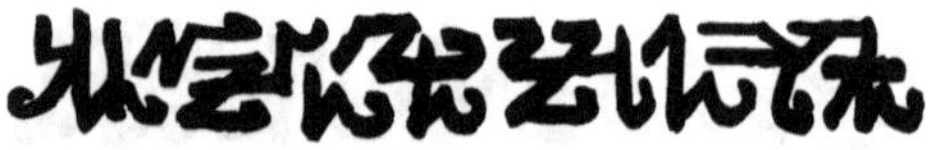

37. The luminosity of no light

+

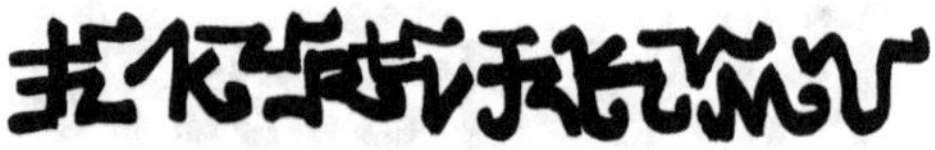

38. Experiencing beyond spatial relationships

+

39. The soundless voice of the One speaking to Itself

+

40. The extraordinary ordinary things of life

+

41. The impossibility of gain and loss

+

42. The opening of the portal of man

+

43. Beyond the unreality of mind

+

44. Creating a surrendered dance of no beginning

+

45. Endless perspective

+

46. The only truth is the new expression of the moment

+

47. Unknowing genius

+

48. Growth as an impossibility

+

49. Moving beyond love to all-encompassing compassion

\+

50. Unlabeled individuation

\+

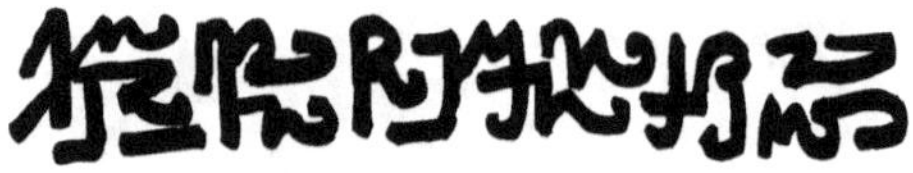

51. Only One expression in existence

\+

52. Removing the screen of life and death

\+

53. The unauthenticity of seeking enlightenment

\+

54. The tyranny of heart's guidance

\+

[symbol]

55. Effortless knowingness

+

[symbol]

56. The healing of the split persona

+

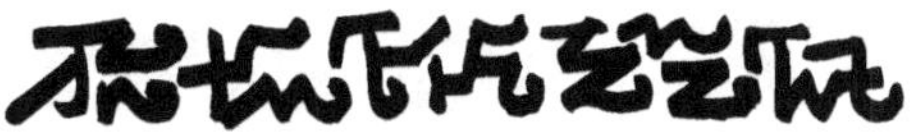

[symbol]

57. Refined experience without the illusion of growth

+

[symbol]

58. Illuminating the shadows of memories

+

[symbol]

59. The elimination of repeating patterns

+

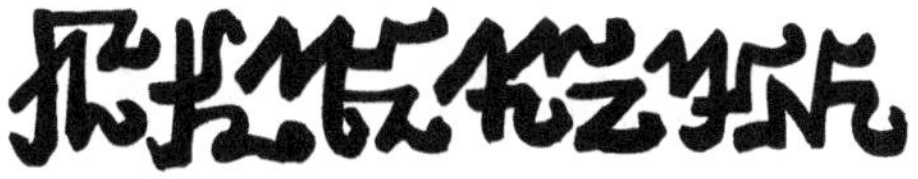

[symbol]

60. The fully awakened choices of emphasis

+

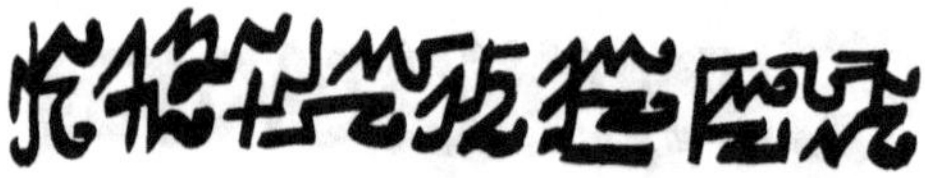

61. The illusion of choice dissolved through surrender

+

62. Incorruptible living through no tones

+

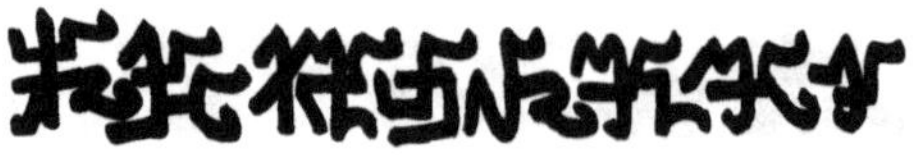

63. Creative games of aware pretending

+

64. Dissolving the screen of life and death

+

65. Unpredictable infallibility

+

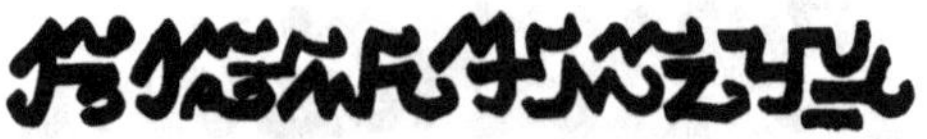

66. Self-genesis instead of procreation

+

67. Diversity through Oneness

\+

68. Free expression that has always been

\+

69. Untold songs of silence to sing in the moment

\+

70. Fulfillment is recognition of the All contained

\+

71. Dissolving the mist of accrual concealing the abundance of All

\+

72. Nothing can be prevented nor begun

\+

73. Accessing depth of being through motionlessness

+

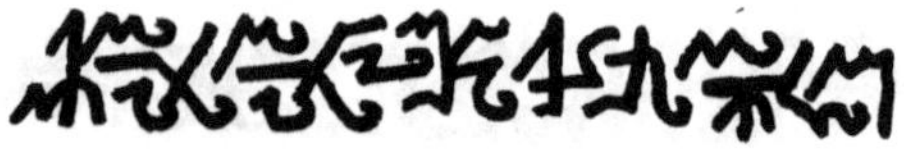

74. The contradiction reveals the perfection

+

75. The dissolving of the tyranny of the real

+

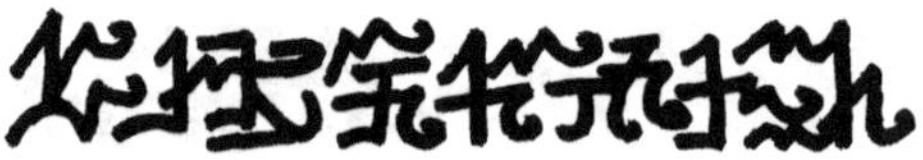

76. Forgotten programs of play remembered

+

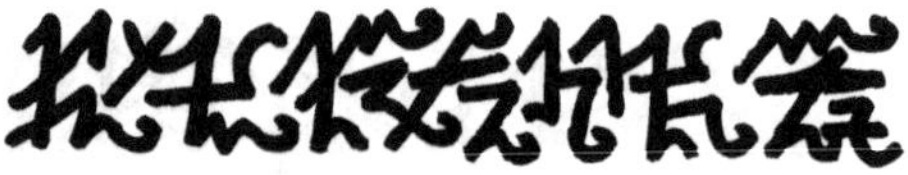

77. The virus of questions removed

+

78. Releasing all contracted focus

+

79. Lightness of release

\+

80. Luminosity of Oneness rediscovered

\+

81. Forgotten beginning re-invented

\+

82. Timeless release of repetition

\+

83. Truth created from eternal expression

\+

84. Erasing the shadows of mysteries

\+

Book I. The Saradesi Records — The Fountain of Youth

[symbols]

85. Bringing enthusiasm to restful repose

+

[symbols]

86. Allowing the gifts we already have to be received

+

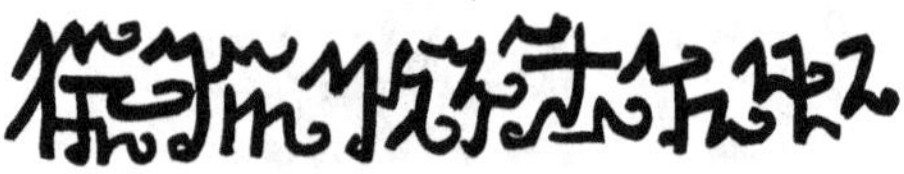

[symbols]

87. Hearing in the breaths between our words

+

[symbols]

88. The self as infinite repository

+

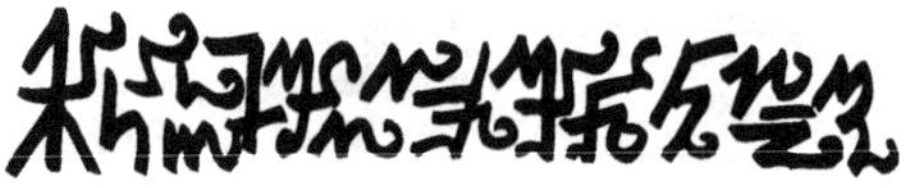

[symbols]

89. Removing the last and first separation

+

[symbols]

90. Changing the game of chasing shadows

+

The Lemurian Science of Immortality

91. Virility reclaimed by remembering its presence

\+

92. Flight of happiness

\+

93. Soaring through the clouds of benevolent life

\+

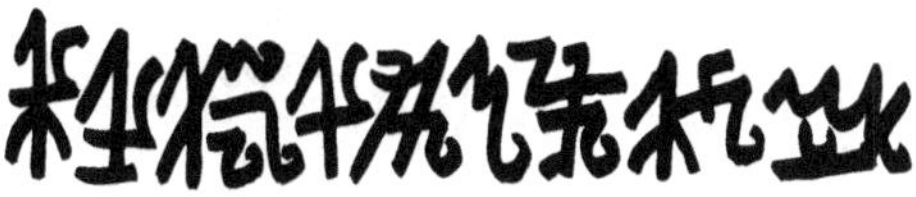

94. The Divine speaking to Itself

\+

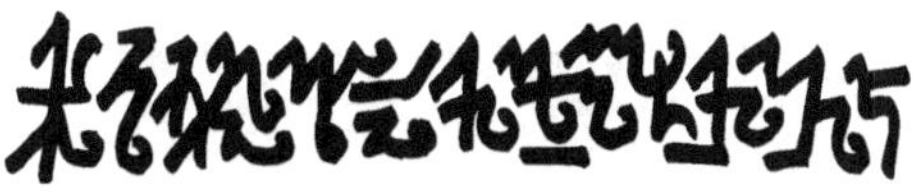

95. The kiss of everlasting life

\+

96. Breaking free from contraction that never existed

\+

97. Knowing that no question has an answer

\+

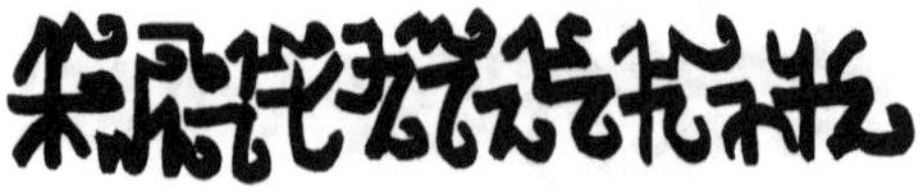

98. Allowing the unexplainable to take us home

\+

99. Dissolving the adventure of life and death

\+

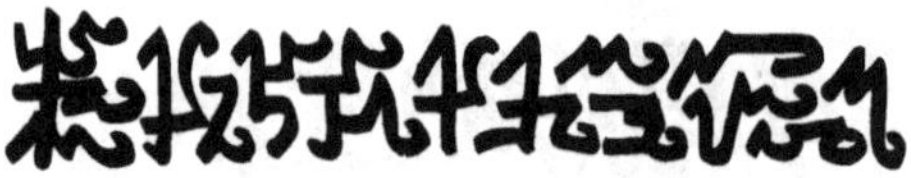

100. Flying into the face of eternity

\+

101. Dismantling the arrogance of controlling mechanisms

\+

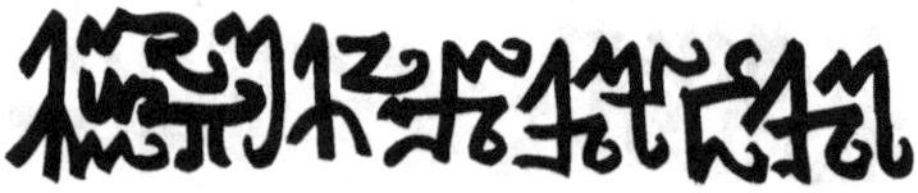

102. Living where unimaginable beauty unfolds

\+

The Lemurian Science of Immortality

103. Free flight of ecstatic creation

\+

104. Knowing the rapture of thought-free existence

\+

105. Unfathomable miracles of silence

\+

106. To infinity's endlessness and back

\+

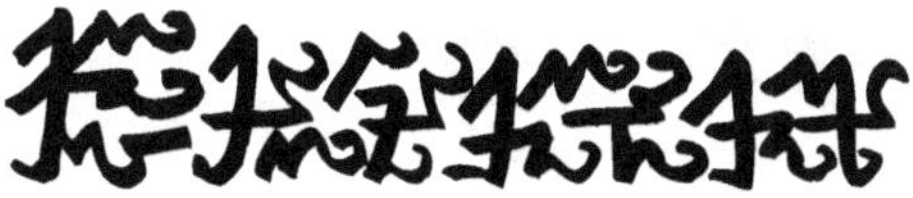

107. The greatest adventure of existence

\+

108. Releasing all self-reflection

\+

109. Relishing the ever-new experience of self

+

110. Emphasizing the carefree enthusiasm of childhood

+

111. Perpetual newness embraced eternally

+

112. Releasing all desire for certainty through trust

+

113. Releasing the barriers of formed formlessness

+

114. The eternal child within the adult

+

115. Experiencing nuances beyond the senses

+

116. Refined self-experience explored

+

117. Beyond the need for abundance

+

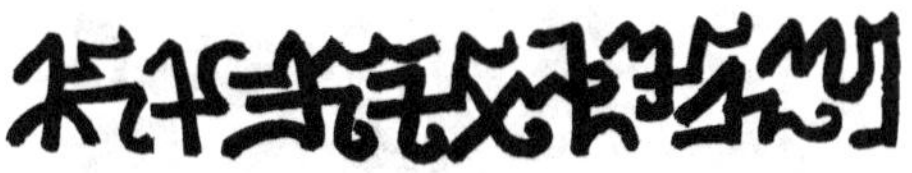

118. Sovereignty as the nature of existence

+

119. Flowering abilities

+

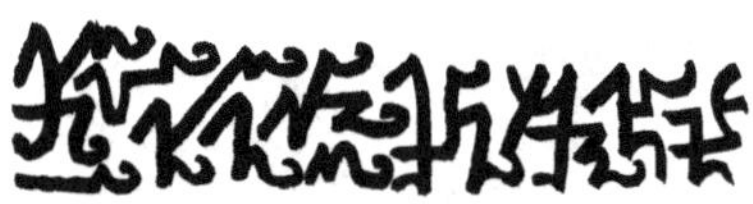

120. Rippling consequences of awakening

+

Book I. The Saradesi Records — The Fountain of Youth

121. Kinship with the natural world

+

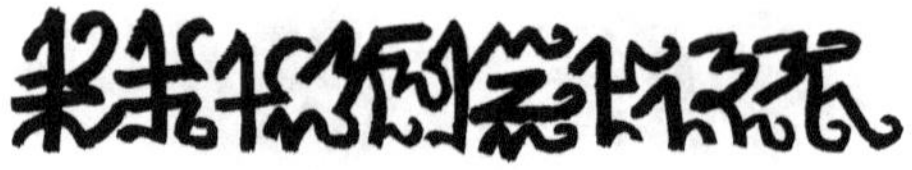

122. The laughter of the cells

+

123. The uncontainment of the All

+

124. Dissolving the impossibility of contraction

+

125. Erasing the messages of the stones

+

126. Hope and mastery unified

+

127. The dissolving of the need to increase

+

128. The holy breath of intention

+

129. Uncovered perfection

+

130. Crossing over non-existent boundaries

+

131. Forgetting old standards of fruitfulness

+

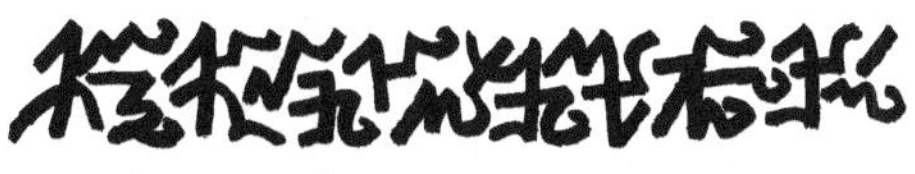

132. Deeply moving appreciation of existence

+

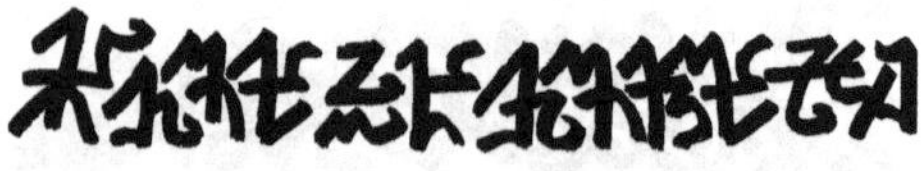

Book I. The Saradesi Records — The Fountain of Youth

133. Being the glow-worm and the starry sky

+

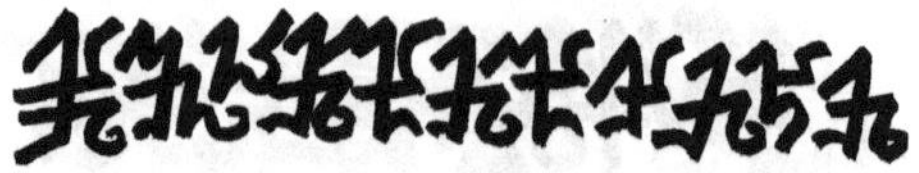

134. Is the one falling through the sky to nowhere, going up or going down?

+

135. Setting nations free through liberating the self

+

136. Breaking the spider web of relationship

+

137. Trusting the spontaneity of fluid expression

+

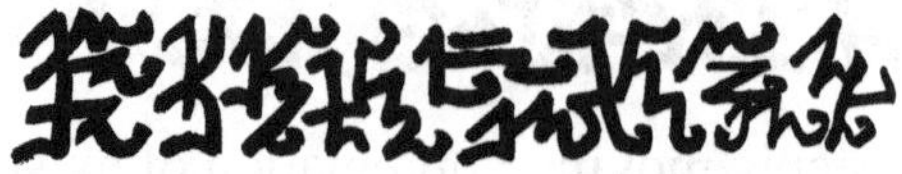

138. Migrating with the swallows within

+

139. Through surrender, embrace the glory

+

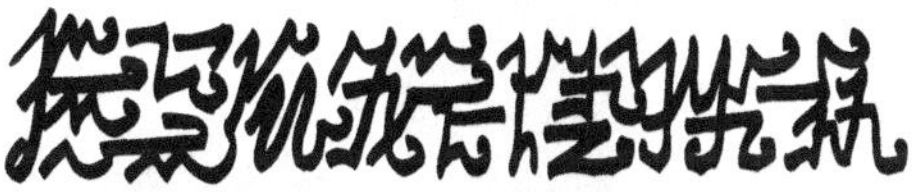

140. From no origin, in surrendered flight, to no destination

+

141. I am free from creation's illusion

+

142. Becoming the unexplainable known

+

143. Nothing to fix, just perfection to see

+

144. Expression and beingness are One

=

Book I. The Saradesi Records — The Fountain of Youth

THE CONCLUSION OF THE 144 PART EQUATION

I am the Paradox
The Paradox am I

The Voice of the Divine Feminine

FROM THE SARADESI TABLETS

*No questions to answer,
nor mysteries to see.*

*Just new appreciation for the
ancient timelessness of my being.*

INTRODUCTION

The masculine is nurtured by the feminine, and the feminine by the masculine. When the dominance of the masculine and its tool of mind suppress the feminine, the body wears down as its self-nourishing system fails.

The imbalance occurs due to biased judgements – valuing the masculine over the feminine. Order is comprised of the structures of time and space, formed as part of the masculine's attempt to organize and control life. The gushing unfolding of life expressing is uncontrollable and beyond the grasp of mind. This is called chaos.

Chaos is viewed with fear as it destructures the sand-castles (the old existing orders) mind has built upon the sands of life.

In our attempt to cling to the masculine, order, it becomes a tyrant that governs our lives, increasing activity and over-riding the voice of the feminine. In the tablets, the voice of the feminine speaks.

THE ATLANTEAN RECORDS OF ORDER AND CHAOS

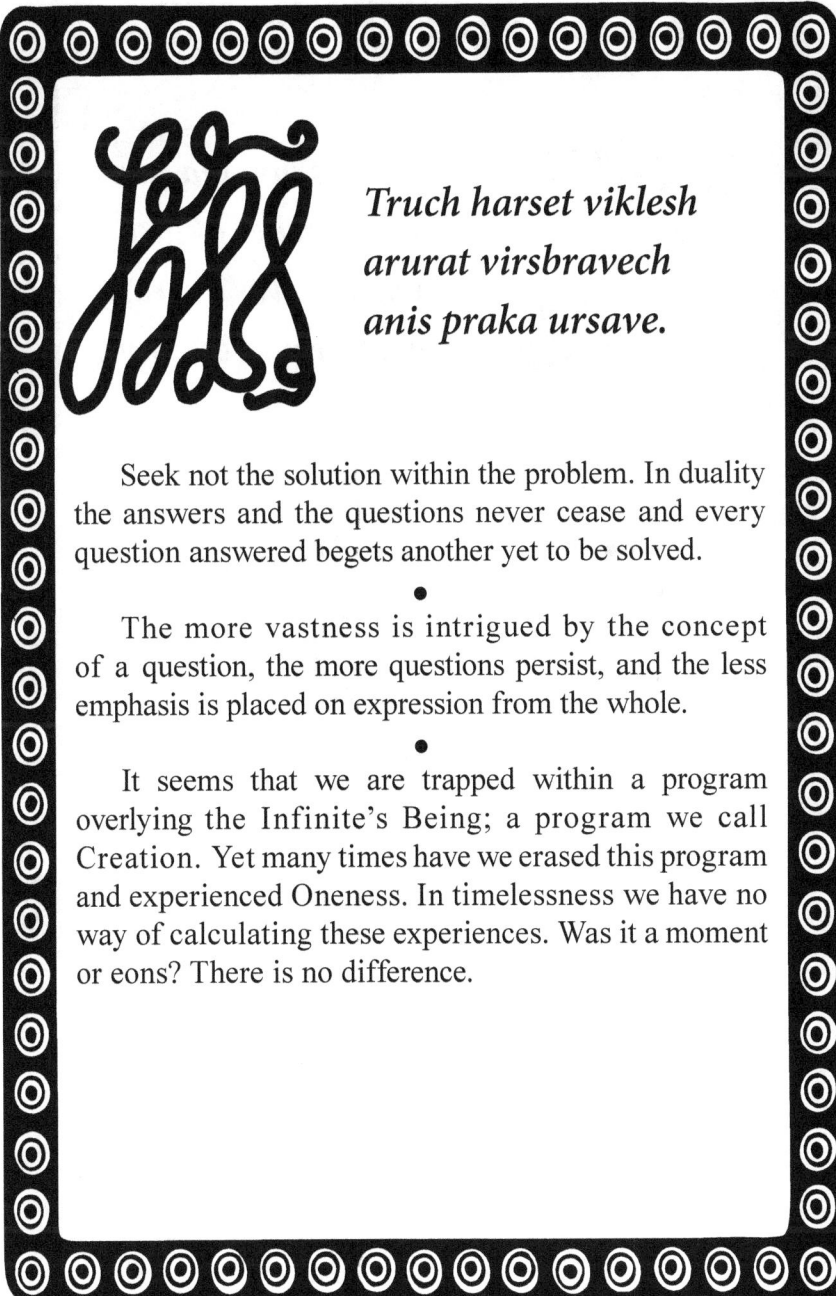

*Truch harset viklesh
arurat virsbravech
anis praka ursave.*

Seek not the solution within the problem. In duality the answers and the questions never cease and every question answered begets another yet to be solved.

•

The more vastness is intrigued by the concept of a question, the more questions persist, and the less emphasis is placed on expression from the whole.

•

It seems that we are trapped within a program overlying the Infinite's Being; a program we call Creation. Yet many times have we erased this program and experienced Oneness. In timelessness we have no way of calculating these experiences. Was it a moment or eons? There is no difference.

Bishanur skavalva urespi minavech sehet aklash vinavach blives araraspi harusut mina veshpavi.

In the dream, can the dreamer remember that between his dreams he has lived a life of awakening? Do we know that between breaths, Oneness was lived in timeless eons?

•

How can we then live while yet in the dream? Remember that naught is as it seems. When we contract, mostly from fear, or try to expand to gain increase, separation occurs and light is split. Let life move through you, do not let opposition arise, that the dream may become one of ease.

•

When we oppose life, duality arises. How does it matter when life's but a dream? To live in oneness while yet in the dream, a lucid dreamer we become: a further step on the journey of awakening and dreaming uniting as one.

*Virenach arsba minavish
herstatve heruvik,
Vibrach aras heresta
Usalvi minha vitrach.*

What are the flesh and the material world, but a program that is temporarily imagined within the Infinite Being?

•

Fear of loss of the flesh keeps the illusion of material life in place. Gross is the environment that is made from the coarseness of matter.

•

Honor the body but eliminate the flesh – the program that binds life into contraction. When the program of matter dissolves, pristineness remains.

•

The eternal can dissolve the unreal by seeing that it never has existed – matter has never in reality existed. Remove it by knowing this.

Book I. The Saradesi Records — The Fountain of Youth

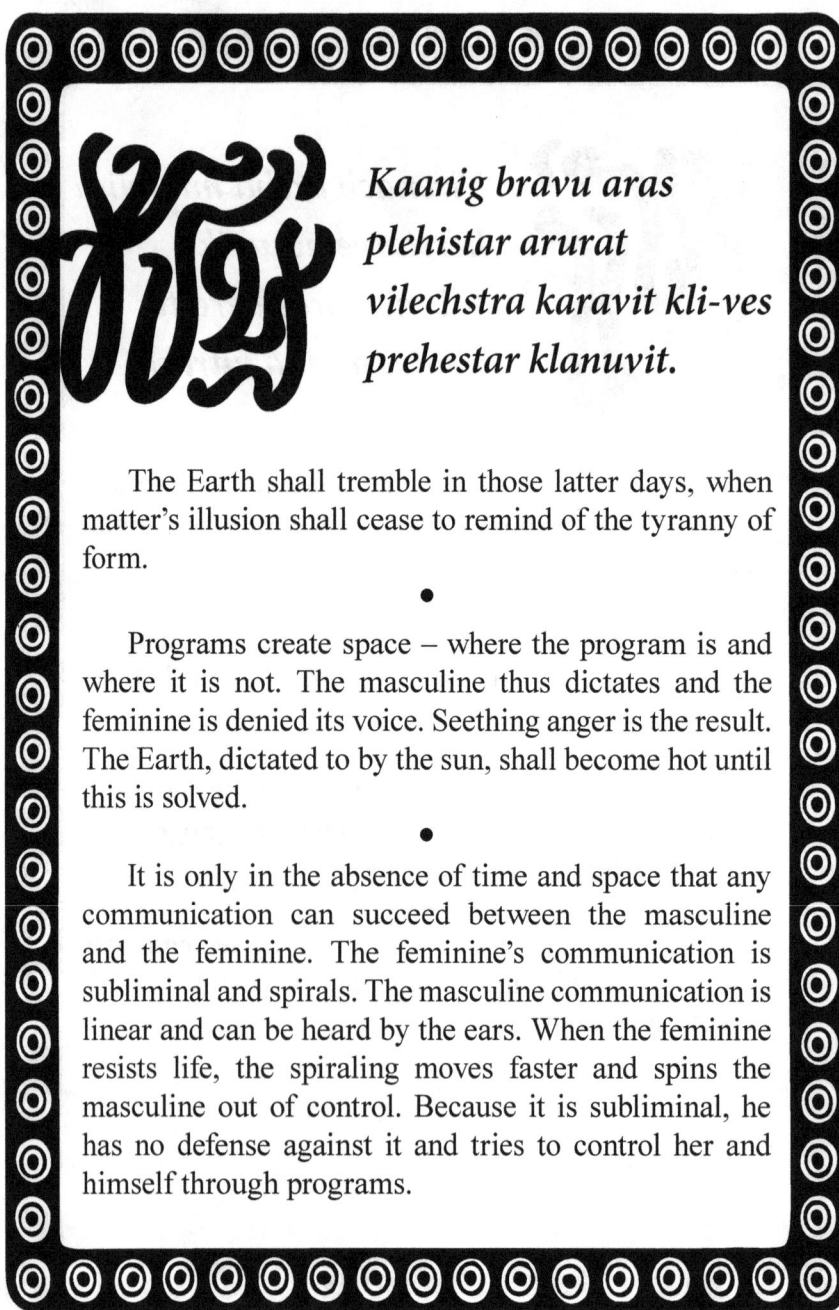

Kaanig bravu aras plehistar arurat vilechstra karavit kli-ves prehestar klanuvit.

The Earth shall tremble in those latter days, when matter's illusion shall cease to remind of the tyranny of form.

•

Programs create space – where the program is and where it is not. The masculine thus dictates and the feminine is denied its voice. Seething anger is the result. The Earth, dictated to by the sun, shall become hot until this is solved.

•

It is only in the absence of time and space that any communication can succeed between the masculine and the feminine. The feminine's communication is subliminal and spirals. The masculine communication is linear and can be heard by the ears. When the feminine resists life, the spiraling moves faster and spins the masculine out of control. Because it is subliminal, he has no defense against it and tries to control her and himself through programs.

Kir savava enech prarech hirusat aklesh vibrach minuvich hirasut esekle unit peras. Uselvi minavit arash pirich hursta vilavet esvi

Geometry is a borrowed relationship from the repository of illusion. From it, the two-dimensional disc of life lived in polarity forms.

•

Why does life turn in cycles that go around and around? Why does awareness spiral as it moves? The feminine spirals as it communicates with the masculine. The masculine hurries the feminine on its way. The masculine uses words to express, the feminine uses sight to sing its silent song.

•

Mostly unheard, the feminine pleads for a journey to have more quality and less speed. When there is no destination, why must there be such haste? Hear between the breaths, the words of the feminine of the self.

THREE TYPES OF AWARENESS

Original Awareness
Movement: It arcs
Originates: Within the Spirit Body
Polarity: Neutral
Location: It moves through all 7 bodies

Inherent Awareness
Movement: A straight line
Originates: Within the Mental Body
Polarity: Masculine
Location: It moves through the 4 lower bodies

Evolving Awareness
Movement: It spirals
Originates: Within the Physical Body
Polarity: Feminine
Location: It moves through the physical body

The three types of awareness create the tube torus of the Infinite and its Creation. It consists of trillions of arcing spirals propelling away from and returning to Source or originating point.

Excerpt from *Journey to the Heart of God*.

The Lemurian Science of Immortality

*Siret akla misuranech vibret arat arakle.
Viranat sabi herustu.*

Why must I be hurried when there is nowhere to go? No destination exists.

•

Kunat harsta arakle vibravech uruva ninus aresta. Arak plihet vibrat hurvastu minurech. Pliva ukret bilasut.

•

To the masculine, my spinning dance seems as madness. To me, hurrying in a directionless existence does. Let sanity come through Oneness.

•

Pluhuvabit ares arechva misut nanes harusta. Kirat haravit aklach blihuvat.

•

Let our joining put an end to opposition within the self. Let it bring still motion of peace.

BOOK II

The Lemurian Tablets of Life and Death

POWER SOURCE OF THE ALCHEMISTS

Our joining forms high alchemy through which both are lifted into exalted Oneness. Both shall know the rapture of dissolving into Infinite existence.

Almine

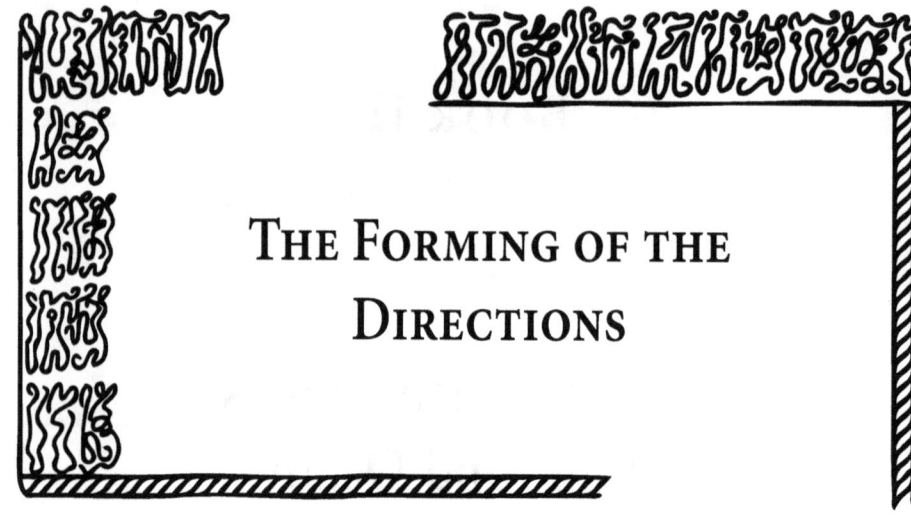

The Forming of the Directions

To the one bound by directions, the moment seems etched in stone, creating a past.

To the one who knows only boundlessness, the moment passes like a finger through the air, leaving no trace.

Almine

The Epic Tale of Gilhamet

THE LEMURIAN TALE
OF HOW LIFE BEGAN

A thriving paradise, the Infinite envisioned
A true reflection of Itself
Thus the beginning of creation was conceived
The tale of which we tell

A single image it would be, that transforms eternally
A smoothly evolving unfolding, to delight the Infinite Being
Sound and imagery combined as one, to be heard as well as seen
A spontaneously evolving tale that unfolds eternally

A screen was created upon which the play could take place
Thus boundaries appeared and an imagined space
Like a moment of time within eternity formed,
Separation's illusion was born

Within Its creative space, the One as the many expressed
Great joy was felt when the play began;
of the dawn of Creation we tell
Upon the screen, in vibrant scenes
Moving images could be seen

Lemurian Writing – 2nd Cycle

As the babe, cradled and content, slumbers and plays in his crib
When life began, innocent it was, much like a babe it lived
Like an infant, the cosmos was steeped in bliss
Intoxicating it was, and so it became addicted to this

When addiction arises, life cannot thrive
Parts cannot develop and get left behind
The microcosm of the macrocosm has always been humankind
Thus throughout ages gone by, addiction among men you'll find

What was not foreseen in this imaginary play
Is that parts of the images would wither away
Limited resources are the result of confines
Wherever a boundary is, limitation you'll find

When resources dwindled because addiction arose
The part of the inner child, which is of the masculine composed
Withered and waned because its environment changed
Frequencies were lost, the inner young boy needed to be sustained

One hundred and forty-four frequencies of the adventurous life
Were gone, and life was seen as a journey of strife
Half of the cosmos's inner child died
The illusion of loss arose; the remaining inner child was terrified

The blue rays of light lost part of its hue
The corresponding tones of the cosmos changed too
The Song of Life in the cosmos became out of tune
To prevent further loss, the inner warrior wanted to do

The inner warrior became driven to produce
A source of energy and life-force they could use
The personalities of the cosmos, he tried to persuade
To move on a journey – themselves to save

Movement brought energy, but in a deep inactivity the inner child lay
The warrior knew that more would perish if for the child they did wait
Because of the trauma, the child was afraid
Who knew what in the unknown journey did await

The child was abandoned along the journey's way
More and more of the inner pieces behind did stay
For few could sustain the frantic pace
For faster did the warrior travel as the child wasted away

And thus ascension and descension cycles arose
A secondary source of resources now did grow
Polarity there was as poles moved apart
The pulsation between them a dynamic energy source imparts

From the separation of poles, shadows are formed
From the unyielded potential, were they born
Potential is only available when oneness is lived
Not when poles pull apart and duality is birthed

The tones of the cosmos are meant to be
Playing in turn, to produce a cosmic melody
But when parts of life are left along the way
The notes or cosmic sound chambers where they are, partially play

Discordance results, which brings disease
The cosmos has had diseased frequencies
Manic and depressed, having abandoned itself
Cosmic conditions reflected within humanity as well

The wasting disease[5] among humanity spread
This disease is by self-abandonment fed
Many burdens are carried through man's archetypal role
But man also has the power to make the cosmos whole

Let now within man, the hundred and forty-four frequencies
Of the adventurous life, once more resurrected be
That the full expression of the inner child may be freed
That healing may come to cosmic life finally

---

5 Cancer.

The Frequencies of Adventure

Contemplate these frequencies and, taking a few at a time, incorporate them into your daily life.

1. *Plechba-minesut*

Expression of unsurpassed skills

2. *Vribach-arakla*

Boundaryless living

3. *Pribes-peleshut*

Boundless resources

4. *Klusarech-viresba*

Creative zeal

5. *Subahet-misenat*

Joyous exploration

6. *Kirsata-eres*

Innovative play

7. *Vribak-barus*

Self-enjoyment

8. *Kelsech-harasta*

Awareness of possibilities

9. Ku-urevit-ares

Creative solutions

10. Mespa-blu-ak

Self-trusting abilities

11. Bribravek-huspa

Magical encounters

12. Melch-kerevek-asabu

Garden of delights

13. *Klisparet-haranat*

Expected miracles

14. *Vrispek-pruhat*

Abounding magic

15. *Mesh-kelenuk*

Loving support

16. *Suvit-arasta*

Confident exploration

17. Urch-manek

Knowing the benevolence of life

18. Suvit-helshta-arunek

Triumphant journey

19. Krihat-elsech-vena

Illuminated play

20. Prubis-haresta

Uncovered perfection

21. *Vela-valesna*

Uncovering hidden treasures

22. *Briberesnet-harsta*

Unmeasured wealth

23. *Kerlahus-preva*

Deep satisfaction

24. *Erk-nanasit*

Nurtured abilities

25. *Hersta-ubravit*

Readiness to be amused

26. *Mu-uhuruch-nesta*

Playful laughter

27. *Vri-baranit-kelechva*

Interactive enjoyment

28. *Vilsh-astahit-melekna*

Cooperative ventures

29. Kustanarak

Amusing perspective

30. Usach-bilestra

Agreeable reciprocity

31. Simanet-hustava

Surrendered flow

32. Vri-avalesva-nachvi

Fluid adaptability

33. *Sabahut-minash*

Oneness with nature

34. *Kuvilavat-miset*

Glad expectations

35. *Asatvi-misaklet*

Fulfilled journey

36. *Bliheresta-meskanut*

Freedom from beliefs

37. *Esavit-kerasnu*

Unbounded self-expression

38. *Usach-biharut*

Knowing self-worth

39. *Klibavat-nusket*

Unencumbered play

40. *Arsach-misbahut*

Lightness of being

41. Plibarut-arkla

Flights of fancy

42. Rutva-plihasbaset

Light-hearted enjoyment

43. Verspahut-arasach

Gentle harmlessness

44. Lutba-spertl-huk

Sensitive inclusiveness

45. Mishete-nanenuk

Profound peace

46. Vrisach-mashmanet

Deep inner-knowingness

47. Kasanis-irklavut

Reverence in expression

48. Mespa-sutra-vilesva

Awe-inspiring recognition

49. Ark-panahut

Enchanting wonderment

50. Sihet-eleskla

Authentic individuality

51. Bribech-eretu

Heartfelt self-discovery

52. Mish-hasvavat-artuhet

Contented aloneness

53. Kerasut-milavech

Deep, abiding At-Oneness

54. Usba-hersetu

Wondrous childhood

55. Kusit-merklavet

Generous contributions

56. Harasta-subahut

Innate consideration

57. Velspa-mutreknut

Serendipitous surprises

58. Utre-belechsnu

Enthusiastic participation in life

59. Kesetra-viresta

Uncovered mysteries

60. Usuch-plibavet

Infallible quests

61. *Rektanut-skibahut*

Agendaless endeavors

62. *Lusenech-ureta*

Lighthearted achievements

63. *Mesevis-aresta*

Confident self-expression

64. *Plibaret-mishpa*

Carefree unselfconsciousness

65. *Nutsarut-plavesba*

Respect for all life

66. *Kestra-mananuch*

Unconditioned behavior

67. *Kuvis-pererut*

Effortless knowing

68. *Klanavit-hersta*

Surrendered living

69. *Speneret-aresta*

Fluid responsiveness to the Song of Life

70. *Vavis-plehatuk*

Vibrancy in expression

71. *Nuselvi-prachbavat*

Joyful disposition

72. *Husel-nanasvi*

The miraculous life

73. Kasanus-preha

Creations of elegant grace

74. Vu-elesatvi

Appreciation of beauty

75. Beles-ustahit

Seeing life's purity

76. Kluset-manesvi

Knowing the perfection

77. *Rutva-pelesut*

Seeing behind the appearances

78. *Nuruk-asbave*

Unblemishable refinement

79. *Kirseta-prahut*

Embracing the Real

80. *Blubaves-erkta*

Inter-dimensional communication

81. Klubaret-mispave

Living the life of the Magical Child

82. Arat-unutvreba

Omni-sensory perception

83. Vruhas-asakla

Effortless accomplishment

84. Erch-manuhet

Embracing the miraculous

85. Visat-plivreba

Incorruptible purity

86. Asanet-useta

Self-referring approval

87. Brihanat-steleva

Empathic compassion

88. Karitna-usa

All-encompassing kindness

89. Prihava-viranit

Living from the Infinite Self

90. Ekta-bruhasprahit

Independent At-Oneness

91. Karet-ertklava

Exciting encounters with the Hidden Realms

92. Hirsat-minavi

Abiding self-curiosity

93. Stahas-plihanur

Harmonious integration

94. Erkta-plubavus

Dynamic balance

95. Maspe-uset-harsta

Fulfilled desires

96. Bribavach-mishatu

Indomitable freedom

97. Uklet-baretvi

Uninterrupted childhood

98. Mechbahur-sabanut

Fluid acknowledgement of newness

99. Mechatu-unevis

Cooperating with the flow of life

100. Krivahet-mishmanech

Absolute clarity of discernment

101. *Suversata-erechsa*

Truth in expression

102. *Kribarut-huves*

Flawless choices

103. *Kesna-elsbavik*

Complete timelessness

104. *Hisanet-iliskla*

Knowing endless options

105. Vibanut-vilista

Being home for the self

106. Usba-plesbahur

Flying on wings of hopeful aspirations

107. Erech-nusavrit

Being rooted within the contentment of beingness

108. Ilskla-brivanus

Rarified appreciation of life

109. Puhuranat-alsvi

Empathic inclusiveness with all life-forms

110. Keret-atur-unas

Embracing unknowing experience

111. Ski-arat-platahur

Mindless genius

112. Vrihabat-skluva

Integrated consideration

113. Virshprahet-nanachsku

Eliminating reference points

114. Bi-ertanis-pelesta

Exciting quality of the journey

115. Vibrehut-mineska

No point of arrival

116. Usekmanut-vileshvu

The sage within the child

117. Rutva-ersklehur

Excellence beyond imaginings

118. Britvret-sku-anit

Artistry in expression

119. Harsta-esenut

Horizonless life

120. Mishet-anat

Uncompromising integrity

121. Klubis-arsenat

Caressing tenderness

122. Klavahis-menesta

Jubilant celebration

123. Ruktretprahut-eresta

In-depth awareness

124. Vrivet-elsavi

Choices of joyousness

125. *Karstana-bravik*

Delightful criteria

126. *Mechbrabanut-hursta*

Unprecedented delight

127. *Uset-meshenech*

Living in rapture

128. *Rekpa-alstravar*

Complete self-presence

129. Verek-harsanat

The elimination of the null-point and still-point

130. Upret-blavanit

Feeling at home in spacelessness

131. Subahech-manavut

The abundant life

132. Kuret-artrava

Receiving bounteous supply

133. Keleset-misaruch

Receptivity of life's bounty

134. Blibesh-arat

Embracing the unknowable

135. Uset-mileset

Self-sovereign participation

136. Virskla-harspanut

Ecstatic discovery of boundless life

137. Utret-karch-anas

Full cooperation with the dance of life

138. Brivanut-sitreha

Guidance through surrender

139. Kelsech-manuhis

The embrace of Infinite support

140. Sukbata-visenit

Self-renewal through incorruptibility

141. Arkla-harusit

A shadowless life of no opposites

142. Visenut-kasavi

Fun-filled laughter

143. Ekvrahit-arsta

Flourishing life

144. Plibavech-isenut

Incorruptible Oneness

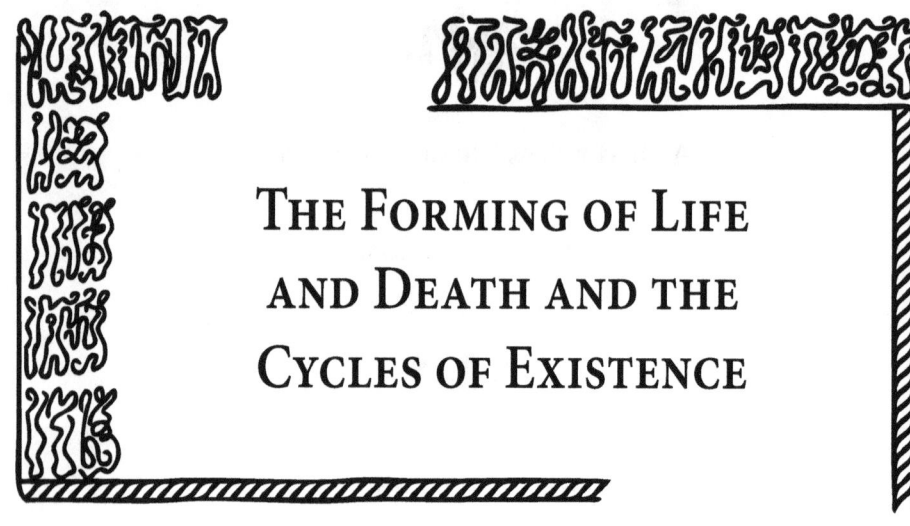

THE FORMING OF LIFE AND DEATH AND THE CYCLES OF EXISTENCE

Who dares to cross
To touch nothingness
To lose the embrace of the cold
stillness in exchange
For a stretch into within ...

Yolanda Ackles, Maryland

The Forming of Life and Death

The image of Creation that was supposed to move
No longer had an unfoldment that was smooth
The unfoldment started and stopped and interrupted the flow
Thus life remained stuck and did not grow

The arrested development affected all beings
Over and over they lived the same scenes
The melody too of the cosmic tones
Played over and over the same notes

Beginnings and endings now came to be
Death and birth came to humanity
Cycles of life from these interruptions were born
The illusions of loss too were formed

The creational cycles like vast moments in a line
In their procession created linear time
Great resources it took to keep such illusions in place
Illusions of death and time and space

The more resources dwindled, the more the warrior's haste
Increased until life moved at a fast pace
Great stress on the fragile parts of Creation was placed
The more were left behind on the warrior's way

The cycles of light ascended by means of luminosity
But could only go so far before life descended to depths of frequency
Wherever we went, we had already been
Each time we entered a cycle's space we left more debris

Layers of meshes, of belief systems comprised
Of world views and programs made by creatures' minds
Gave specific qualities to these cycles of life
The natures they were called, dictating the lives of humankind

The meshes were shadows – one of the illusions of life
Few understand how shadows bring opposition and strife
When that which is one, by beliefs is treated as opposite poles
The fabric of existence tears and forms a hole

A space is opened by polarity and a matrix is born
A protective layer, so it does not spread, around the hole is formed
The shadow forms a mesh or a grid
That artificially the hole may be filled

The shadow, like a thorn in the flesh
Seeks resolution for itself, which is the mesh
It opposes the life from which the polarity came
Thus strife enters our lives and losses and gains

There must be benefit of generated resources from polarity, some may say
But for the gain of resources there is a price to pay
From multiple journeys through a specific space
The layers of grids grow thicker, impeding the way

Inertia decrees that life must constantly be fed
For if it is not, there will be death
Inertia results when self-regeneration is not there
With debris in the way, energy cannot pulse from poles across the tear

The layers of depths that form the natures of humanity
Impede our journey with belief systems of antiquity
The amygdala is the nature's gateway to the brain
The animal instinctive reactions to stimuli come that way

Fools react while masters from stillness respond
Masterful inclinations are over-ridden by the amygdala's emergency response
In our sacred places where truth-seekers dwell
We learn to recognize the animalistic natures well

For in this way, they do not take us by surprise
These animal natures are flawed perceptions in disguise
A time will come in a distant day
When the three illusions that keep them in place will be done away

Note: Number 1 of the Animal Natures is the deepest, most repressed nature; number 24 has formed most recently and is the most likely to come to the surface.

The 24 Animalistic Natures of Man

1. Tasmanian Wolf – self-destructiveness, self-sabotaging

2. Wooly Mammoth – unfriendliness, hostility, short-temperedness

3. Mastedon – tribalism, cruelty

4. Tortoise – protectiveness, isolation

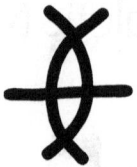

5. Shark – voraciousness, greed

6. Giant Sloth – complacency, laziness, indolence, stubbornness

7. Armadillo – self-centeredness, ego-centricity

8. Komodo Dragon (like Iguanas) – hurtfulness, injuriousness

The Lemurian Science of Immortality

9. Barracuda Eel – territorialism

10. Vulture type birds – opportunists, thrive on misfortunes of others

11. Serpent – Underhanded, backstabbing, subversive hostility

12. Elephant – conformity, dependency

Book II: The Lemurian Tablets of Life and Death — Power Source of the Alchemists

13. Hippopotamus – defensiveness, obsessive need to be right

14. Apes – discordance, stridence, disharmony

15. Emperor Penguin – martyrdom, identifying with suffering

16. Inktaku bird (looks like a Puffin) – helplessness, disempowerment

The Lemurian Science of Immortality

17. Scarab/Dung beetle – ineffectiveness, blindness to solutions

18. Stingray – stuck in a rut, lack of innovation

19. Camel – fearing the worst, pessimism

20. Rat – taking without giving, depleting, selfishness

Book II: The Lemurian Tablets of Life and Death — Power Source of the Alchemists

21. Big Cats – pecking order, arrogance, class-consciousness

22. Wild Dogs – destructiveness, disrespect

23. Bear – desire to dominate, seeking control

24. Wolf – creating drama, finding a need for aggression, finding causes to fight for

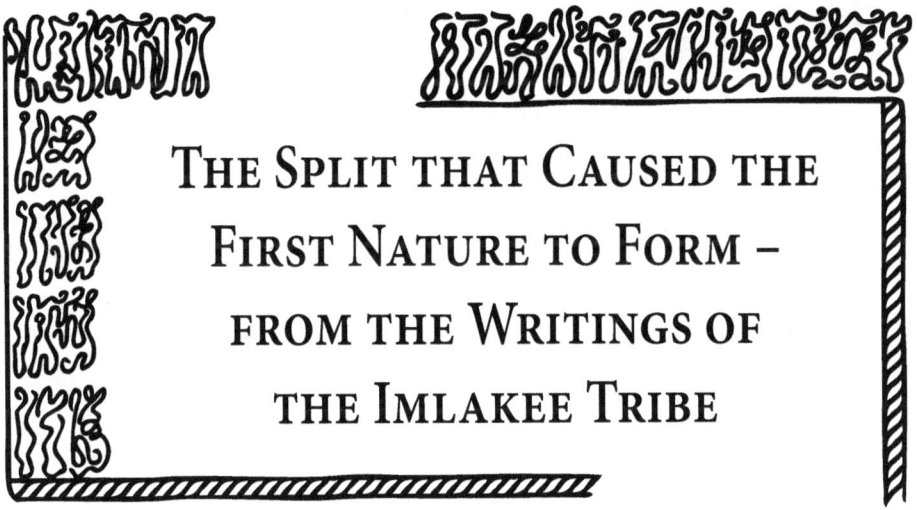

THE SPLIT THAT CAUSED THE FIRST NATURE TO FORM – FROM THE WRITINGS OF THE IMLAKEE TRIBE

To prolong life is no more valuable than to prolong death. Both lose their lustre when viewed against the backdrop of eternity, where existence transcends either state.

Almine

The Split of Black and White Light over Penang, Malaysia

Photo taken by a student during class in Malaysia

According to the writings of the Imlakee – a Northwestern Lemurian tribe who lived in Malaysia – the first split in the human psyche occurred over Penang, Malaysia.

The Writings of the Tribe of the Imlakee

Part of the Tablets of Gilhamet, the Tablets of Life and Death, are written in the tongue of Imlakee – a tribe in the lands of the Northwest[6] of Lemuria.

THE TALE OF THE IMLAKEE

In the land of the Northwest of Shalmali, people lived in harmony with nature. Few were their possessions and the clothes they wore. They were children of the forest and needed none. They called themselves the Imlakee, which means: 'I am you'. They did not have a written language for many thousands of years. Slowly, a few symbols of meaning, written on tree bark, became a written language called Minavech. The word means 'Tongue of Flowers'.

A southern group of people moved to the lands of the Imlakee. The Imlakee called them the Mental Ones – 'Sibu Tarech' – for they had many beliefs, unlike the Imlakee who lived like children ready to explore each day.

The Imlakee arose with the sun and each day greeted the dawn with the words:

Minach imnash uskave

I know nothing

With the growing need of the Mental Ones to control life by creating belief systems, they became trapped and their separation from nature grew. To the Imlakee, nature was a friend, but the Mental Ones sought to control it by building cities to shut it out.

6   Malaysia.

Just as their minds were imprisoned by their beliefs, so their bodies became entrapped by their cities. The Imlakee could feel the burden this unnatural way of life was to the land. They sang songs to comfort the land but it groaned from the destruction of the forests to make way for the cities.

The Imlakee could see that a big wave from the ocean would come to try and wash the land clean. They moved inland to the mountains to prepare for the day. But first they did send a delegation to the Mental Ones to tell them of what was to come. The Mental Ones could not recognize truth. Their words were rejected.

The Imlakee were rejected with arrogance. Many perished when the wave came, because of such foolishness. The Imlakee felt anger in their hearts at the destruction of the forests by the hands of the Mental Ones and the natural disaster it brought to the land.

In the aftermath of the wave, a more terrible tragedy came: the light tore and split into black light and white light. The Imlakee became invisible to the Mental Ones. The hidden kingdoms too, became invisible to many of the people on Earth. Man became lonely and cut off, living in the white light. The Imlakee and the fairies still live in the subtle black light, waiting for the split to heal.

The Urban Jungle

QUESTIONS FOR THE INFINITE

Q. What can be done to escape from the city jungle's noise? We need it to live; yet it strangles our authenticity with its claws.
A. What is a city but the belief systems of your mind externalized? It cannot live without you, nor can it contain you when you live from the vastness of your being.

Q. But is a natural environment not to be preferred? Are cities not to the Earth, a scourge?
A. Nothing can exist that does not a purpose serve. What is disacknowledged persists and what you grudgingly endure is strengthened.

Q. Pray, tell us then what good can come from artificiality? What purpose does it serve, this man-made urban complexity?
A. Neither simplicity, nor complexity exists in unfolding life. When you live in Oneness, there are no opposites. Incubation chambers of specific qualities and self-knowledge, are the man-made structures of which you speak.

Q. But do they not also breed illusion and depravity?
A. What is illusion but a detour that leads to pristine realities? Does the experience of 'what is not' then not ultimately bring understanding of that which is real? Can the light be defined other than by shadow? Yet one is valued and the other not.

THE URBAN JUNGLE

*Boredom has been the cause
of much non-life-enhancing conduct.*

*It is the state we enter into when
we think we have no options.*

*Existence abounds with endless options.
The adventure of life is to find them.*

Almine

Q. But the detour through illusion brings pain. Is there not a better way, perception to gain?
A. Within the One Life, nothing can be lost or gained. There is no difference in value between a life of joy or one of pain. Beyond seeming opposites, lies Infinite Beingness that cannot be explained.

Q. Is the one who chooses simplicity, to live in nature's harmony, not more able to experience joyous states?
A. Yes, but a city dweller is locked in life's passionate embrace. Joy and passion are opposite poles and play in these opposing lifestyles emphasized roles.

Q. How do we reconcile these two poles? How do we find freedom wherever we go?
A. In the city, find a life of elegant simplicity. Do not engage in its many games of insanity. In nature is great diversity. In awareness of its many nuances, co-operate with it in humility.

The city is a wild animal. At night I hear him growl. His red eyes flash on street corners. On pillar legs he prowls.

Translated from an Afrikaans poem by Uys Krige

THE NOISE FACTOR

Q. How can it be equal in ultimate benefit, when the sounds of nature like a dulcet symphony seem and man-made noise like an invasion feels?

A. Noise is an irritant – that is sure. Some make use of what others grudgingly endure. The irritant brings divine discontent that causes man to reach for a better way of life. This in some creates the desire to achieve, while in others it causes strife.

Q. What of one who in nature lives? Does this not great contentment give?

A. This is so, and thus achievement is less; stagnation may set in for one who in beingness rests.

Q. How do we cope where noise is prevalent? Does it not create egoic mind and disturb innocence?

A. The key to not having these undesirable states occur is to see the body as a pliable field and the noise as passing through. When noise is resisted because it is seen as detracting from the quality of life, tension forms and thoughts do too.

Q. How is this achieved, please tell?

A. By living from the greater self. In your vastness, you are the bustle of the city and the peace of the countryside. That which you wish to experience, emphasize inside. Is it rejuvenation you seek; then emphasize the dawn. Practice living from your vast expanse and life becomes so much more.

LIGHT AND SHADOW

Q. Where does shadow come from? How can it exist when the perfection of the Infinite is all there is?
A. The perfection of the Infinite is only partially expressed by Its creations. No matter how much is expressed, more awaits for interpretation. This is held as potential, which is unaccessed frequency and light. A shadow it casts as the Infinite illuminates life.

Q. Then how do we access potential and eliminate the shadows it casts?
A. The more life is lived in opposites, the less ability to interpret Oneness there is. Know there cannot be bad or good in the Indivisible Perfection that exists; that value judgments may cease and duality disappear.

Q. Is it good or bad, that which lies beyond the disc of life? The unyielded potential, does it still apply?
A. It is where the gifts you seek, and unimagined qualities, lie hidden waiting to be retrieved.

Q. Like information kept in cyberspace, off the computer screen? How do we enlarge the screen that the information may more easily be seen?
A. To one who lives in egocentricity and in polarity, the screen of life small shall be, not able to interpret Infinite luminosity.

Q. If we want to interpret untapped potential, what method shall we use? Other than to eliminate polarity, what can we do?
A. As the past 12 reincarnation cycles speak to us through symbols in dreams (and in our daily lives) if we know that life is more than it seems, so the deeper cycles of your lives speak in Dreaming Poetry, where images of profound beauty bestow their qualities.

Q. What of the depths of animal instinctual natures? How do they communicate?
A. Through Poetry of Dreaming too, but a slight difference will be detected by you: more like a riddle do they seem, having a slightly mental quality. They are designed to confuse the mind that it may release its tyranny.

Q. To access the natures, is there anything else that we should do?
A. From the Infinite, a set of 24 mazes shall be given to you. But first master the Poetry of Dreaming, before you receive the new.

Q. Then what now of potential, how can it speak to us?
A. Through stories you will receive in the silences of your lives. No analysis is needed for the confinement of your screen comes from your mind. Leave rational cognition behind – the meaning of the stories as a deep feeling you will find.

Q. As we access our potential, how will it affect the rest of life? In doing this for ourselves, will it a great service provide?
A. That is so, for this you must know; many beings of shadow exist. As that which casts the shadow is turned into light, beings of shadow will be changed by this.

Q. What must we know, but did not ask? Please tell us this as well.
A. In the Poetry of Dreaming, much is revealed by that which is not told. So too, the beauty of man through the unexpressed unfolds. By feeling the potential that hides in their gaps, your fellow men you may assist. For in allowing their magnificent potential to change your life, it is set free by this.

> *My breath is the autumn wind that blows the russet leaves*
> *My soul, like the ocean in unfathomed eternal motion heaves*
> *New as the perpetual dawn, I am all, yet none of these.*

THE POETRY OF DREAMING
VERSES FOR THE CITY

1. The city is like a wild animal: At night, I hear him growl. His red eyes flash on street corners. On pillar legs he prowls.

2. The crazy man screams at passers-by; they say he's lost his mind. Is this not what sages seek; as enlightenment for humankind?

3. In an overgrown garden, in the full moon light, an old woman dances – the one they call insane. Outside a pub, where liquor flows, students do the same.

TRANSLATION FROM THE LEMURIAN TABLETS

The Nature of the Wolf – the most recent that has formed
Like all twenty-three other natures
From a grid like a spiderweb has been born
Twenty-four spiderwebs made by man's minds
Born of the self-reflections of humankind

The spiderwebs are mazes that entangle the way
They are not works of art – of resistance to life, come they
Underneath them all, in each dream cycle we find
An exquisite labyrinth designed to enhance the way

As a timing-mechanism, by the Infinite were they made
That life could be enjoyed as it enacts the play
Move now the mazes, immediately out of the way
With frequency you can do it, in an Alchemical way

The alchemical equation, through the Poetry of the Dream you'll find
Do this and remove great density from the path of humankind

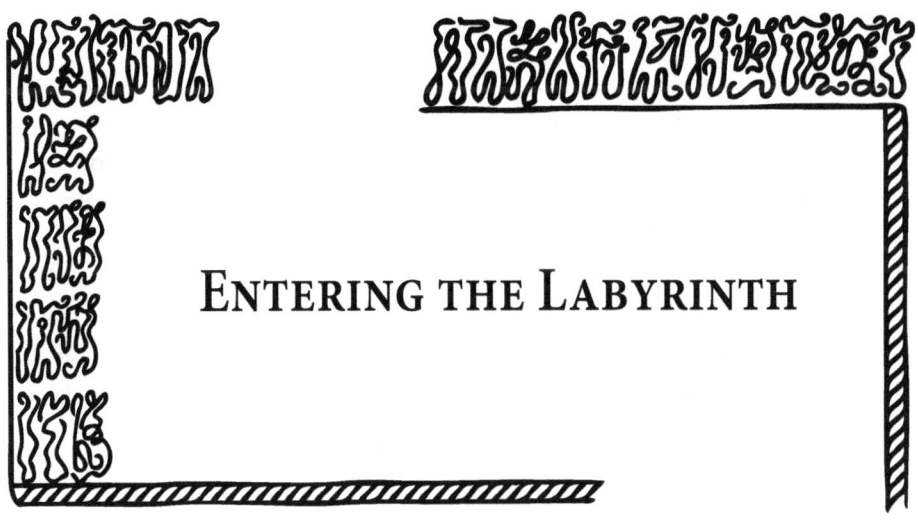

Entering the Labyrinth

When the mazes formed, blindness was born.
Man could no longer see the Embodiment
of the Infinite Being.

Almine

The Deep Layers of the Natures of Man Speak

There is a variation found in the style of the Poetry of Dreaming when it comes to the language of the natures of man: It becomes more cerebral – a riddle of the eternal paradox that is meant to confound the mind. The poetry of the previous incarnational cycles, on the other hand, is a captured moment of exquisite imagery.

The imagery is meant to give a feeling; the riddle is meant to bring insights through effortless knowing – the insights we missed because of belief systems during successive journeys through specific incarnational cycles.

The wolf pup chases its tail – round and around it goes.

The Cosmos in circles travels, around like a fish in a bowl.

The Poetry of Dreaming to know the Insights of the Natures

1. Around a fire on a full moon night, he dances till a sheen on his copper skin glistens in the light. His hair black as the wing of a crow, his feathers quiver and shake. He dances till his spirit with the eagle takes flight.

2. A pillar-post bed, white linen coverings. White gossamer curtains drift on the sunny morning air. Yellow flowers in a vase spread a delicate fragrance everywhere.

3. A majestic lion with a mighty mane stands on a rocky hill and inspects his domain. In a thorn tree's shade in the heat of the day, the tortoise in his shell sleeps the hot hours away.

4. "Let me tell you my adventures, beloved, in far away lands," whisper the enamored waves, as they rush to embrace the warm sand.

5. Reflected in the gleam of the falcon's eye, is the setting sun on the water and the apricot sky.

6. The olive trees bend and twist like hoary wrestlers in the wind. The plaintive wind loudly complains that forever he must roam, never to know the feeling of roots, never to have a home.

7. Down grassy hills, amidst apple trees, laughing children tumble and play. A startled cow urges her calf to run away.

8. A turkey wing, a rattle and sweet-grass smoke proclaim a sacred ceremony, that the spirits may know and gather around the prayers that rise from a pipe's bowl. Up to the Creator's ears they go.

9. A flight with a broken wing, around and around will go – going nowhere while exhaustion grows. Let the masculine be healed and the magic revealed and life's flight of glory unfold.

10. The weary wagon train, on the edge of the plateau, overlooks the fertile valley; the promised land below. A salvo from guns at the setting sun, acknowledges that a miracle has come.

11. In a majestic array and a colorful display, the peacock spreads his tail. In unabashed glory, in the sun's last rays, he bids a flamboyant farewell to the day.

12. Wind chimes sound in the gentle breeze. Peace flows through the limbs of the old oak tree.

13. The marlin leaps to catch the moon. The stars laugh at such sport, startling the sleepy spring geese, resting like a feathered flotilla on their way home.

14. The chrysalis opens. Wings spread to dry. The colors of life call the dragonfly into the sky.

15. A flock of wild turkeys roaming over harvested fields. A school of fish, a flock of geese – many eyes, yet one being.

16. The green of the leaves and the fragrant breeze, delights a caterpillar in the tree. A trail of enjoyment wherever he's been, he leaves behind him though unseen.

17. In the dew of the morning, to the warbler's delight, the magnolia bud trembles and unfurls velvet pink petals to the early dawn sky.

18. Through shades of a purple dawn, a formation of ducks quack loudly at the Asian farmer and his mule, plowing the misty farmland.

19. A deep lake cradled in the bosom of the Earth watches in reverent silence as a new day births over an autumn farm.

20. With his hand paused on the goblet, he listens to the perfect succession of silver notes from a distant flute on the evening air.

21. The night falls onto the land with a sigh of silence. The mountains reach for the mystery of the silver moon, adrift in an endless sky.

22. From its confines, with a burst of faith, the dandelion's down flies free upon the wind. Fanned by miracles, it floats to new beginnings.

23. Heavy with seduction, the intoxicating fragrance of pink lilies insinuates itself through the garden. A blue jay pauses to drink in the heady bliss.

24. "I cannot see or hear the whisperings of my being," you say. "Encased in flesh, with others' phrases, my own soul is unknown." Why then, I ask, must words describe the buttery nuances of your bliss? That which ripples like sun rays through your being and enfolds you in Infinite peace? That which is real cannot be described, yet neither should it be denied because it cannot be defined.

HOW TO INTERPRET THE NON-COGNITIVE MESSAGES

1. Take time to feel the feelings the images evoke – this is most important. Even if you cannot cognitively understand any of it, by allowing yourself to feel the poetry of the images it will beneficially alter your life.

2. Some images come as a sentence or an instruction and they say what they mean. Others are symbolic. The symbolic ones will not be presented like a piece of poetry but rather as a prosaic image. Someone is getting a promotion or buying new clothes for instance, rather than a captured moment of perfection. The direct communications speak for themselves; symbolic ones can be looked up as dream symbols.[7]

---

7   See *Labyrinth of the Moon*.

The Gaps that Formed the Mazes — As given through the Poetry of Dreaming

The mazes are layers of scar tissue that formed to protect the gaps in our ability to express the Song or Dance of Life. To find the insightful knowingness of the gap releases the need for the maze to exist.

THE GAPS IN PERCEPTION THAT FORMED THE MAZES

1. Not valuing the limitation of humanness.
2. Not valuing the creative works of man's hands.
3. Thinking life is controllable by taking it at face value through selective vision.
4. Strengthening self-importance by valuing external accomplishments.
5. The formation and value judgments of the real and unreal.
6. Feeling deprived because of emphasized qualities of others when seeing them as separate from ourselves.
7. Protectiveness is the result of feeling that imperfection can exist within the One Life.
8. Feeling unsupported, man sees the need to gather allies for support, such as the tribe.
9. The masculine's need to know and understand has incapacitated the adventure of life, causing an exhausting, circuitous journey.
10. Because of being exhausted by his opposition to life, man invented the concept of a point of arrival.

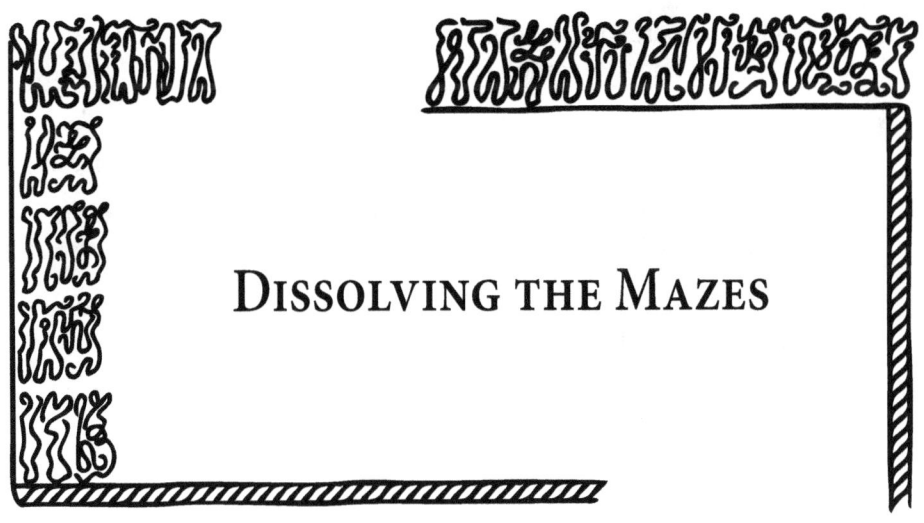

Dissolving the Mazes

Where the mind encounters an unfathomable mystery that creates a gap in its carefully structured belief systems, it reaches for an illusion to bridge the hole.

Almine

11. The linear construction of the mutual mazes gave rise to the concepts of linear becomings, beginnings and endings, which we eulogized.

12. The misperception arose that effort and rewards correlate; that one has to earn joy.

13. The flow of past standards as criteria of self-evaluation arose. It is folly to think the little self can have success or failures.

14. Outside promptings became a guidance system when the inner life became impoverished.

15. Self-pity and self-importance arose through us representing either one pole or the other; as we look to the opposite pole, we see our lack and to compensate, we then over-value the pole we represent.

16. We value external, tangible gifts more when in fact, the unseen ones have an exponential impact.

17. We have forgotten to see that all things are new at all times, eternally.

18. We have forgotten to find adventure everywhere.

19. All discovery is self-discovery and all appreciation is self-appreciation, yet we think them to be outside of ourselves.

20. We have forgotten to see all moments as perfect – like a row of perfectly played notes in the song of life.

21. We reach for an external mystery when we forget we are the never-ending mystery.

22. Parenting became a form of enslavement by placing conditioning and belief systems on our children.

23. The only love affair can be with life. By forgetting that, we transpose it onto another, unfairly making them our whole life.

24. That which is real cannot be described, nor should it be ignored.

QUESTIONS FOR THE INFINITE

Q. How shall we know what was missed that produced these gaps that formed the mazes so long ago?
A. Ask instead what caused the inability in the first place. Eternally, an incapacity exists for a creation, which represents a nuance of Infinite expression, to interpret the whole.

Q. So ever-new potential and shadows form as life ongoing flows? To bring enlightenment then is like carrying water in a sieve! We try for naught to make it lighter by the conscious lives we live.
A. The tools I give can access, in a non-cognitive way, the new potential that is formed every day; the old of the past must dissolve away. Potential henceforth, when its usefulness is outlived, may not stay.

Q. What happens to the lives of the many and to our own, as more and more this technique is known?
A. The screen of life enlarges and all species' capacities grow. Your consciousness and alignment shall more alignment show; more miracles shall show in the lives of your loved ones and your own.

Q. Please tell me how, this I must know.
A. Deep into silence you must go. Once you are there, a tool I will show: a magic box all your own. Get to know it very well. Then use it in a way of which I will tell:

DAILY MEDITATION TO ACCESS NEW POTENTIAL

1. Spend time in a preparatory meditation going deep into silence, just to get to know the feeling or sight of your box (which is just a useful toy to achieve communication with that which lies outside of life's accessibility). Once you are able to call up your box in meditation, proceed as follows.

2. Imagine the box lid opening as you go into deep meditation. Inside is a projector that projects a scene for you to look at. Write it down.

3. Go back into meditation and wait for a second scene. Write it down. Continue in this way until the images stop. Come out of meditation.

4. Try to recall the feelings and any additional background impressions of the scenes to flesh them out and make them more complete.

5. Try and connect as many of these short scenes into a story or several little pieces of a story. You can make up small connective links.

6. Do this daily and the stories will become more coherent. They may however stay unlike the logic-based, cerebral stories we are used to. If you have not been able to connect the scenes, this is still successful.

It is not in connecting the dots of the scenes that makes this technique successful, but in the non-cognitive knowingness that floods through (and reaches us at a deep level) between the images. The changes brought about by doing this meditation as a daily practice will become obvious in subtle but profound ways.

MESSAGES FROM UNTAPPED POTENTIAL

1. The cosmos we are in is like a blue dwarf. We are as a cosmos surrounded by an orange sun. When the blue sun expands into the orange sun, we become an enlarged white giant, having the full spectrum of light to express Infinite life.

2. The children shall become the elders in their ability to access unyielded potential through imagery.

3. The blue ball, which is our Cosmos, is a dense sphere that does not allow light through – its surface is a mirror. Life in the surrounding orange 'sun' has contracted into egocentricity because of its obsessive encounter with its reflection. This has put pressure on the cosmos, like coal being squeezed into a diamond.

4. Over-inflated mirrored distortions gave the masculine self-importance; the reducing images of the feminine made it feel less – compounded by the shadows cast by unaccessed potential from having to express from limited color ranges and reduced screen sizes caused by contractions.

5. The way to get out of old ruts has been to reboot the computer – this is done by dumping all old memories and programs. But the computer then reprograms itself. The pineal needs to be reprogrammed not to repeat old cycles through hormones and the bloodstream.

6. Within the screen of life, certain colors should be emphasized to produce, through certain qualities, the breaking down of man-made mazes.

7. Three hearts need to become purple: the heart chakra of man, the central crystal or heart of the Earth (Klanivik) and the cosmos itself.

8. All descension and ascension cycles are to become one. The Hidden Kingdoms are to become physical, staying hidden through magic if they choose.

9. All natures are to become one, by dissolving all previous grids or mazes. Animals will become more conscious.

10. The frontal lobes of humanity are to be fully activated so that images from the Infinite can be clearly seen. The 3rd eye chakra is to be changed to silver.

11. The most recently formed grid of the wolf promotes the desire to create drama. This must be replaced with the quality of peaceful exploration of the self in the adventure of unfolding life. This must be emphasized in the Inner Warrior, Inner Sage and the masculine (little boy) aspect of the Inner Child.

12. The receiving area for the unaccessed potential is the solar plexus. As we use the imagery of the stories, it grows larger until the receiving area includes the entire body.

13. The third chakra becomes orange. It is a gateway to the potential within. This was obscured before by the grids of the natures, thus we reached for it without the cosmos. There is no within or without.

14. Learning to feed off the new daily potential by going within will reverse aging, which happens because of leakages through 'holes of untapped potential' in the body.

15. The voice of all beings needs to be recalibrated anew all the time, to express newly accessed potential. Combined with new truth it renews the body. Forgetting what we think we know assists this.

16. When the voice is recalibrated to express accessed potential, it combines with new truth alchemically to break down old matrices and grids, and silences the will of the little, egoic self.

17. The cycles of ascension and descension, and the natures and potentials surrounding the cosmos, are the 4 directions that must combine to birth a life of no opposites.

18. Neither expansion nor contraction exists. It is only the game of changing focus to bring playful variety to the adventure of life.
19. Questions based on a premise of illusions create insecurity and more questions. Questions based on what is indivisible and real, enhance the adventure.
20. The sub-personalities and the masculine and the feminine will always be ill or broken – they are based on separation.
21. The dissolving of separate sub-personalities can only happen when all are equally expressing. The nurturer is expressing but does not feel heard. It can provide the spiritual nourishment we seek without.
22. The feminine's domain is darkness, a black slate that can hold many more colors than a white slate. White light is confined to 3 primary colors. The masculine programs life to fear darkness and value light, ignoring and devaluing the feminine.
23. The mazes, the cycles of life, the natures – all were created as a method of control and security by masculine sub-personalities. The feminine had no part in creating the computer screen. The Labyrinths and yogas were given as keys to get life out of the screen.
24. The ancient contentment of the endless depths, like the ocean we come home to, like the land as old as the Earth: these are the feminine foundations of our being inviting us, through daily communications of imagery and poetry, to get to know it until we live immersed in it. Then we will know we are home.
25. The feminine is the foundation of life – from it, in a series of 3 schisms, the masculine warrior, elder and masculine of the inner child split off. Their activity has seemed like madness to the feminine, which withdrew from it as the masculine went around and around.

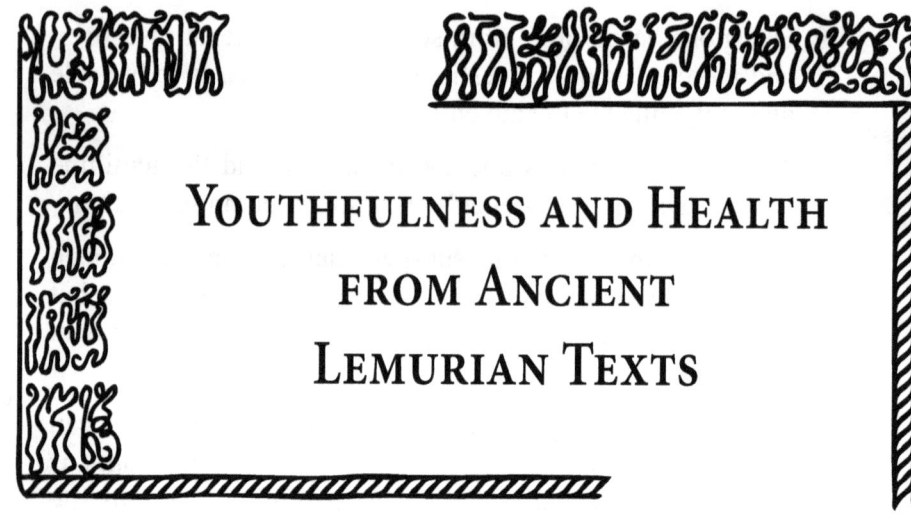

Youthfulness and Health from Ancient Lemurian Texts

*Live now from that part of you which
has neither a beginning nor an end.
Only beyond opposites shall
you find authenticity.*

Almine

The Scroll of Namud

Excerpt from the Scroll of Namud

TRANSLATION

From the Motherland[8] we call Shalmali, great wisdom was spread to the many people of the Earth. Wise masters called Nagas[9], which means 'gates of wisdom', were sent to teach. They took tablets of wisdom with them and separated into groups of two, copying these tablets so that they could share them with different people.

They taught the Naga language to all in walled temples called Chaldi or Kaldi (meaning 'walls'). Seven sets of holy records were taken through high mountains (the Himalayas) to the land of Monassa (India) and placed in Kaldi temples in seven cities. They became known as holy or Rishi cities ... Devi Satva Yoga was designed to create enlightenment by opening various sets of gates in the human body.[10]

Minikva ares prihat uruva nachte.

Within man are the answers to the starry skies.

---

8   Lemuria.
9   Called Naguals or Nacaals in some tongues.
10 See *Irash Satva Yoga*, *Shrihat Satva Yoga* and *Saradesi Satva Yoga*.

Almine Receives Various Scrolls to Translate
(As seen in interdimensional photography)

Photo by Shelley, Canada

Taken in Sedona while Almine was teaching.
Note the scrolls on her head, January 2010.

Almine Receives Various Scrolls to Translate (continued)

Photo by Shelley, Canada

The Scroll of Namud rests on Almine's head.
Taken in Tampa, Florida while teaching, February 2010.

Translation From the Lemurian Scrolls

Eranachvi Erashkla Uharuvit Nenastu Subleva
Close down the matrices and divisions of mind

The matrices and grids you will come to see
Have kept the cosmic creatures' sanity
There are few who can stand to see the Goddess's luminosity
The grids have provided a thickening shield

As brighter and brighter the Goddess came to be
How can the Cosmos finally ready be
The glory of the Goddess to see?
With no mind and high frequency

QUESTIONS FOR THE INFINITE

Q. When and how can we raise the frequency high enough to be able to 'raise the veil' or dissolve the grids and matrices, without many beings going insane?
A. There is no time, but there is a sequence that must be in place: as you know, the cosmos raised in light that culminated in its ascension.

Q. Yes, in the first week of December 2009.
A. The Cosmos had been there many times before but had then always then gone into a frequency ascension – what you call a 'descension,' in which there was black light …

Q. The Yin and Yang symbol illustrates this.
A. Yes. When light grew, frequency decreased and vice versa, as is the case with all polar opposites. For the cosmos to finally leave the

cosmic incubation chamber mind had created for it, the frequency and light have to be equally bright and at optimum levels ...

Q. Which seems impossible according to the laws of polarity.
A. Yes, to create the impossible, the lightbearers split themselves – leaving their light-filled selves at the apex of the white light ascension and also ascended in the parallel black light reality, raising the frequency. When this is also brought to its apex, the two realities cancel one another out by combining. This reveals a much higher level of life in which the masculine and feminine can enter into oneness.

Q. And lightbearers are no longer split ... where are we now on reaching the frequency apex?
A. Three more raises, like half tones on the piano.

Q. What must we do to achieve the first one?
A. I will show you and your class how to experience that which lies beyond emotion, which is the frequency of desire ... experience it as the next step.

Note from Almine
My class and I experienced an almost indescribable feeling of completeness and fulfilled rapture. We felt an experience of such refinement that common emotions seemed coarse by comparison.

> *The nuances of cosmic life played across the receptive strings of my soul with such exquisite clarity that I felt my being explode in rapture across the cosmos.*

Notes from the students
"I saw Almine change into a being both male and female – then to a beautiful older gentleman – a little bent over, but very elegant."

K. C.

"When I saw you speak, your 'bodily' form was fluid – changing from one form to another very rapidly toward the end. I have observed this before – the last time I heard you speak, the sequence was: angel, youth, beauty, tall being with gold light and a crown over your head. Also you changed during the talk from small to large – basically it was like a dance."

Katherine

"During the class of Almine in Sedona, I saw her shape-shift from old to young, large to small – many times."

Michael

Excerpts from Lemurian Records

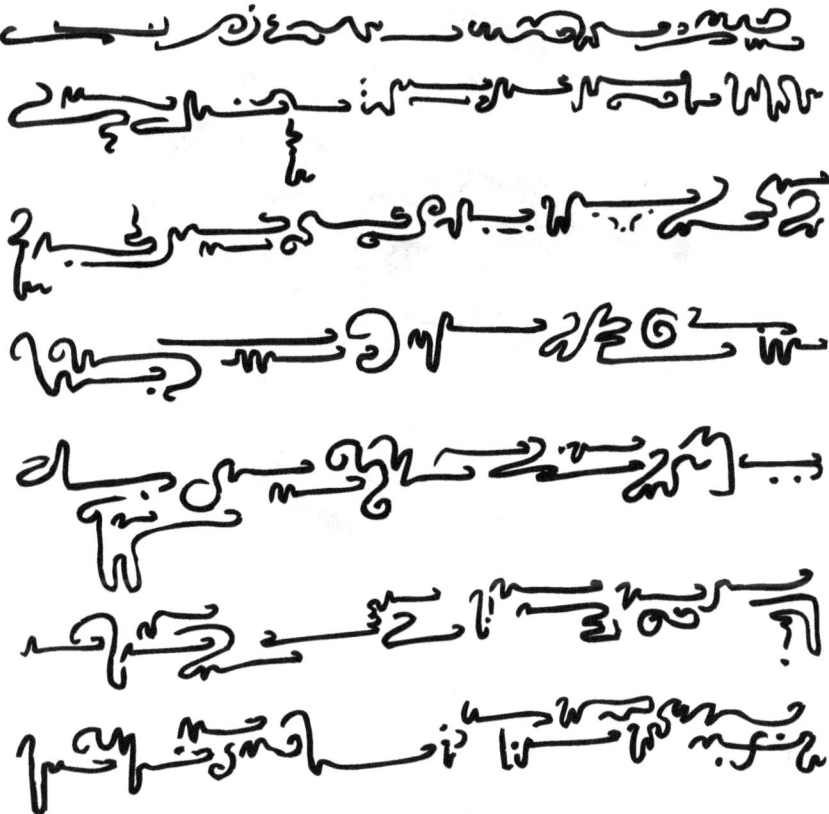

EXCERPT 1

Clearing Memory Implants at all Levels

Those steeped in dogma and dwelling in monasteries
Have bowed down in worship, while mystics have been free
But value there is in honoring that which lies beyond the maze
It widens our vision and heals our gaze.

EXCERPT 2

Size is Nothing to the Infinite

What is it that will happen when the masculine and feminine unite?
The joining of Creation's body and soul, which is Eternal Life.

EXCERPT 3

Spontaneous Composition through Emphases

Nature is the feminine creation, the opposite to the creations of mind
The animals are a bridge between nature and humankind.
They will help us see with our skin, where our eyes are blind
They are our allies in remembering how to bypass mind.

The animals that most fearsome seem when captured in a maze
Are endowed with great properties within the black light to find their way.

EXCERPT 4

The Purified Cave of Forgotten Treasures

The feminine can only see the wide vista of life
The masculine by his vision of details is confined
Both must be joined and omni-perspectives be birthed
Like a falcon's eyes see in depth and in width.

EXCERPT 5

The Purified Dynamic Balance of Spirit

The veil of illusion that life is confined
Created the concept of self-reliance designed by mind
"Self-reliance is isolation," the tortoise sighs
Replaced with Oneness, life will thrive.

EXCERPT 6

Entering the Timeless Garden of Self

Black wolf whispers: "Hear and see with your skin, then
the journey into the black light of the Goddess can begin."
Aging comes from separative senses' lies.
They are ineffective ways of knowing life.
They take more than they provide.

EXCERPT 7

Karakarana-Una

Great self-abandonment occurred when the
masculine and feminine split apart
Thus in our masculine cosmos, holes came into its heart
The holes were filled with entities, occupying the empty space

The conscience formed, as high mind it is known
And wild woman in the direction of below
The masculine part of the Inner Child
Artificially formed, for the feminine part was left behind.

EXCERPT 8

Restoring the Full Magic of Existence

Elephant carries a message from ancient times
An alchemical equation awaits as higher in frequency you climb

The Equation of the Elephant

![glyph]

Multi-perspectives through Omni-sensory perception

+

![glyph]

The ability to experience tones visually

+

![glyph]

The intoxicating experience of the Oneness of light and frequency

=

![glyph]

The mutually fulfilling union of the masculine and feminine

Perpetual Rejuvenation through Mastering Opposites

The art of rejuvenation, unknown to the masses, has long been practiced, with varying degrees of success, in the mystery schools of the world. Locked away from corrupting influences of man, these mystics have attempted to disengage from the grid that programs the death and life cycles of man.

These practitioners of the rejuvenation methods, well-kept secrets of the ancients, were sometimes encountered by outsiders, who attested to the virility and strength of the masters even at very advanced ages.

There are three stages of overcoming death and decay known through the ages, each mastering one of the stages of linear change. In order to understand them, we must first be aware that life spirals around and around a triangle of three very distinct stages of transformation, transmutation and transfiguration.

1. **Transformation:** This stage takes place when we are in the process of shedding the old and the obsolete. Growth is slow during this stage because it follows a mathematical sequence (the Fibonacci sequence). Life is the largest stage an individual lives that is transformational. Life is lived in white light.

2. **Transmutation:** This stage has leveraged growth, because it is alchemical in nature, following an alchemical sequence, not a mathematical one. Death (or life in the spirit world) represents the largest transmutational cycle. It is lived in black, or etheric, light.

3. **Transfiguration:** Having become more etheric, and having risen in frequency during the previous stage, the transfiguration

of the individual is the inevitable next stage. The body and its fields transfigure[11] in order to hold more light to match the increased frequency. The largest transfigurational stage is ascension. The individuation and self-awareness is retained, but the form is not necessarily kept. These realms have what is known as grey light (traditionally known as 'Heaven' because of having no burdens commonly associated with physicality – the sensual joys are also not present and growth is almost non-existent).

In mastering transformation (the physical), life can become prolonged for about 10,000 years. It is known as immortality.

In mastering transmutation (the soul), life can be prolonged to about 100,000 years. It is known as incorruptibility.

In mastering transfiguration (the spirit), life can be continually rejuvenated. It is known as perpetual rejuvenation.

The Principles of Rejuvenation

1. **Immortality**

    - As part of mastering transformation (which purifies by getting rid of the old), the master of immortality must delay the ultimate purification rite – death.

    - In a heightened state of awareness, the master watches every detail of his or her life for mirrors of what needs to be purified within, constantly living in a state of overcoming blind spots and growing in perception.

    - Perception increase feeds the individual more and more light, which feeds the body resources (prolonging life) but depletes the soul. The call of the soul for the individual to come to the spirit world (death) becomes more and more

---

[11] See the free online course with video, *Pathways to Ascension,* Day 4: "Power and Ascension," www.spiritualjourneys.com/ascension/power/

feeble.

- Because two opposite poles, such as life and death, can only delay alternating their expression so long before stagnation sets in, life must eventually yield to death.

2. **Incorruptibility**

    - When life has been lived and soul demands its share, either in increments (aging) or in a lump sum (death), the incorruptible master changes the rules of the game.

    - When the paradigm of life is a small one, the game takes place in a small circle – the poles are close together and they have smaller intervals between alternating dominance. When death comes knocking, the incorruptible master increases the parameter of the paradigm he or she is living.

    - Increased frequency yields perception and increased perception yields frequency. The master now enters into intense frequencies of love, praise and gratitude, or sees more than ever before.

    - The parameter can only be pushed so far until, eventually, death must be able to get its share of existence. The only way to sidestep this eventual limit (like a rubber band that can stretch no further), is to move into transfiguration.

3. **Perpetual Rejuvenation**

    - Transfiguration moves between form and formlessness, a principle that can be utilized to 'rebirth' the actual physical body over and over again.

    - When the body alternates between form and formlessness, instead of life and death, it has chosen another opposite. Death now has no opposite to pulse with – a necessary energy source for opposites – and yet again grows weaker.

- Death now creates opposition (from our 'higher' self in the spirit world) to wear us down. It then promises us 'rest' in the after-life.
- The transfigurational sequence is 1, 0, ∅, -1, ∅, 0, 1 (the positive numbers being formed life and the negative numbers formlessness).
- The master uses perception to make a massive leap out of his paradigm (circle of expression) so that it far exceeds the level of frequency. The master then goes into complete emptiness and allows his stretched perception to shoot back, thrusting him into the formlessness of spirit.
- Because the solidity of physical life requires a large amount of resources to maintain itself, life in formlessness leaves more resources available and accessible. As the master returns, he rejuvenates his body through the resources he brings with him.
- Only a few seconds may have passed in physical life but the master may have rested for months in the timelessness of spirit. As he increases in mastery, the ability to change the appearance of his form may also be achieved.

These techniques no longer belong to the hidden teachings of mystery schools. The fear that they can be misused is unfounded since they are based on the increase of pure frequencies and light. They are where they belong: as the birthright of man.

The soul can be nourished by incorporating the principles of the heart into our everyday life; through the holy marriage of matter and soul.

The Ways in Which the Archetypal Animals Assist us to Find our Way in the Black Frequency and Black Light

1. Tasmanian Wolf – instantaneous self-birthing
2. Wooly Mammoth – storytelling of the psyche's non-cognitive messages
3. Mastedon – complete trust in the perfection of the self and its beingness
4. Tortoise/turtle – graceful ease of expressing in the masculine and the feminine
5. Shark – fearless self-exploration
6. Giant Sloth – transcending illusions
7. Armadillo – Mystical journeys
8. Komodo Dragon – at ease with boldly and authentically expressing
9. Barracuda Eel – the peace of timelessness
10. Vulture – accessing omni-perspectives
11. Serpent – the instant flowering of abundant fertility
12. Elephant – seeing the greater perfection
13. Apes – adventuresome discoveries of delight
14. Hippopotamus – omni-sensory perception
15. Emperor Penguin – refined enjoyment
16. Inktaku bird – the self-confidence of boundarylessness
17. Scarab/Dung beetle – the ease of spacelessness

18. Stingray – the Magic Restorer
19. Camel – experiencing Indivisible Compassion
20. Rat – the Uncoverer of the Mystery
21. Big Cats – Eternal Rejuvenation
22. Wild Dogs – effortlessly rearranging of circumstances to the highest rapturous delight
23. Bear – the alchemical leveraging to the highest results
24. Wolf – the emitting and receiving of great, glowing luminosity

Pull from the Black Moon Well deep within

Now, use your voice to weave potential sacred water into your skin ...

THE MEDITATION FOR THE RESTORATION OF YOUTH

Place yourself into meditation.

You will be contemplating that which is – Realizations and creating with hope – Visualizations.

Realization 1

   a. Aging comes from cutting ourselves off from Oneness.

   b. Cutting ourselves off from Oneness comes from trying to define life, which creates boundaries of separation.

Visualization 1

   a. See the ocean with a small island. The island has 7 trees on it.

   b. The trees are creations of the island: the sub-personalities of the Inner Child, Nurturer, Elder, Warrior, Above Nature (High mind or conscience), Wild Woman or Wild Man, the Sub-personality of Within.

   c. The island is the Masculine, the ocean is the Feminine.

Realization 2

   a. Because space does not exist, the ocean is in the island and the island is in the ocean.

   b. The island formed because of trying to define.

   c. The sub-personalities are unreal and must dissolve.

   d. The body is the island. The soul is the ocean.

Visualization 2

   a. See yourself sitting on a mountaintop observing the night sky. Observe the trillions of stars through your eyes.

    b. Then close your eyes and observe them through your skin. In your visualization, your skin can see and hear.

    c. Now allow your skin to see the starry skies within your body.

    d. See the skies within and without as liquid.

Realization 3

    a. If there is no space, there is no inside or outside, nor barrier of skin between the two.

    b. Senses help promote the illusion of inside and outside.

    c. Senses only detect the 'outer' partial reality by seeing and hearing only White Light and Frequency. Black Light and Frequency remain subliminal and undetected. The archetypal animals are our inner senses.

Visualization 3

    a. Once more see the starry skies 'within and without' you.

    b. Become aware of the 24 archetypal animals 'within and without.'

    c. Call them by their physical and soul names to come to the skin of your body and

        • Remove all memory of the skin as a barrier or division.

        • Bridge the communication gap between the 'inner and outer'.

    d. Call out these names:

1.	Tasmanian Wolf	Umbatanu
2.	Wooly Mammoth	Suviratanu
3.	Mastedon	Kluvanik
4.	Tortoise	Haratu
5.	Shark	Nanunit

6.	Giant Sloth	Pribatu
7.	Armadillo	Viranet
8.	Komodo Dragon	Kuranetu
9.	Baracuda Eel	Vribanut
10.	Vulture	Kiratu
11.	Serpent	Virista
12.	Elephant	Sukletvranu
13.	Hippopotamus	Piheretu
14.	Apes	Utanavitenu
15.	Emperor Penguin	Plibaruk
16.	Inktaku (Puffin bird)	Nektaranu
17.	Scarab/Dung beetle	Skiharut
18.	Stingray	Virstenut
19.	Camel	Bruherenut
20.	Rat	Asaklenu
21.	Big Cats	Miretanu
22.	Wild Dogs	Vrubitenat
23.	Bear	Arsklanavi
24.	Wolf	Vitrenat

Realization 4

a. With the ocean within the island, with the Cosmos within your body, the only way to differentiate the masculine from the feminine is through his artificial structures and divisions.

b. If those were dissolved, there would be no masculine.

c. Without the masculine, there would be no feminine, for one is defined by the other.

d. What would remain is indivisible androgyny. That which is indivisible is real.

Visualization 4

    a. With your left hand on the Wheel – *The Labyrinth of the Solar Plexus* and your right hand on your solar plexus, see the black waters of the wellspring of your soul pour through your solar plexus, which opens like a doorway.

    b. See it fill your entire body, from your toes and feet, up your legs and to your head. Let it fill every cell – dissolving the cells of the body, the blood, the bones, the teeth – all separate organs and parts.

    c. Continue this until you are a form of black accessible potential. Know that it is perpetually renewed.

Realization 5

    a. As pure potential you can shape-shift your body to any age or shape.

    b. The body as ever-renewing potential that you can express is not subject to aging, illness or death.

    c. Accessible potential is inseparable, luminous compassion.

The Labyrinth of the Solar Plexus

*Weave your dreams and hopes into realities
from the river of the starry skies that flow
through the endlessness of your being*

The Labyrinth of Saradesi – the Fountain of Youth

Travel on its message, ever shifting Sacred Breath
Everywhere you go ...
And continue to forget
Everything you know ...

Alicia

Fragments from the Lemurian Scrolls

1. Creativity is inspired by omni-vision through inner and outer senses combined.
2. Unification is doomed to failure because it is based on the illusion of relationship.
3. Unification reveals the flaws of both parties, whether the unification takes place through sex or otherwise. The process of unification or any other relationship forms a mirror.
4. Consciousness evolves from self-sovereignty to unification to Oneness.
5. Sexuality through genital connection becomes unnecessary when there is Oneness between two people. Any touch can bring a feeling that transcends emotion (for instance passion and joy) to a rapturous fulfillment.
6. The Poetry of Dreaming and Soul Storytelling, that relay the 'stories' of past dream cycles, bring about the unfolding ability to experience omni-sensory capacity.
7. Stories of the Soul or Soul Storytelling, replaces memory with a series of stories. For example, a story about a child being chased by a wolf does not traumatically affect us. If we believe it really happened to us, we may still feel it's effects – for instance, by being frightened of being in nature by ourselves. Since linear time does not exist in reality, neither does the past. If we are influenced by memories, we are influenced by the unreal. In Soul Stories, like the Poetry of Dreaming, we are able to change through the non-cognitive, feminine information in the gaps of the story, as well as the words (cognitive, masculine communication), which tell of insights from previous incarnations. All memories should be treated as 'stories' – Stories of the Soul.

8. Illness is born from the soul and body not communicating. Tension comes from unyielded data.

9. All wish to grow, but where to? There is no point of arrival, nor boundaries to transcend. The increase we seek is to remove the tarnishing of polarity and to restore the greater and indivisible luminosity of the One Life.

10. For many eons the belief has endured that inner guidance is preferable to outer guidance, which comes in the form of signs, synchronicities and symbols in our environment. However, the existence of both inner and outer guidance strengthen the illusion of direction. Surrender instead to the perfection of existence.

Saradesi – The Secrets of Youthening through Androgynous Balance

Ka-ahaneesh kelech prihana uvaveste plihanat useve.

The real cannot be described, yet it is where perpetual rejuvenation lies.

Kelsech usevi manach selvabruk steruch ple-eha unaveshvi skelerut.

The incorruptible has always been, yet is ever newly unfolding.

Selchva minashet ukreva spelavit uklesve mirut etreva sahutbavi.

The body and soul together make immortality, but beyond them lies incorruptibility.

Chanis huraset aklashvi anas uraret kivar aranus.

That which is indivisible cannot be explained nor be defined.

Karushat anes aklat vrabis arunesvi harasat miklavi vabrech kri-uvra-vanet.

Like brilliant feathers through a forest trail, we can but guess at the magnificence of the bird itself.

Rik-varabet eravas uklavavi vribach herustat varablik minesvi arustat harusat miklavi.

All that you think you know must be forgotten if you wish to see a flash of brilliant plumage in flight.

Almine's Note
When life is approached through the combined feminine and masculine and without thinking we know, it becomes like Alice in Wonderland, falling into another world – except this one is not dysfunctional, but truly a wonderland.

THE MEDITATION OF RENEWAL

Place yourself into a deeply relaxed state and in your inner vision see a little boy and a little girl, twins – as they playfully gather treasures that are newly delivered by the ocean's edge. With wonderment a shell is gathered, a shiny pebble, a piece of driftwood ... all is placed in a red bucket. Just observe the sun on the water, little footsteps washed away by the foam, squeals of delight from children's voices ...

Realization 1[12]

  a. Nothing can be retained. Like footsteps in the sand, all washes away.

  b. Our attempt to create continuity through memory requires huge resources as does anything that pits itself against the tides of life.

  c. All aging is the result of attempting to control life, and therefore an unnatural occurrence.

Visualization 1

The sun is setting over the incoming ocean tide. The little boy and girl walk hand in hand away from a beautiful sandcastle adorned with shells, pebbles and other treasures; their faces rosy from the sun, their bodies sandy. They laugh together at two seagulls squabbling over a scrap of food; their red bucket is empty ...

---

12 Take time with each concept and allow them to sink in.

Realization 2

a. Memory is a defense mechanism that causes linear time. Linear time robs the body's youth. Tension forms in the skin and body by living in linear time.

b. The defenses that hold onto memory occur because of thinking we are a unit, separate from the whole, and that we have to fend for ourselves:

- By mapping our journey through life by remembered relationships so that we will find our way.
- By being ready with past references for the unknown future.

Visualization 2

The children go into a little patch of woodlands, laying crumbs down to find their way out again. The birds eat the crumbs. When they try to retrace their steps, they cannot. Instead they have a wonderful adventure pretending to be lost, until their mother calls them home ...

Realization 3

c. By building the future on, and defining ourselves by memories, we go around and around in mediocrity, bound by past standards.

d. Memories create personalities, and they in turn, lock physical degeneration in place.

e. Identity is static, and static programs are anomalies that do not belong in the ever new unfolding of existence.

Visualization 3

Place your left hand on the Wheel – *Labyrinth of Renewal* (see page 229) and your right hand on your heart.

See the mask of your skin melt away with its signs of wear and tear. See another, newer you revealed as the old peels away. Do this as many times as it takes to reveal a youthful, new you in luminous perfection. Realize that you have no skin left. Your body is a pliable field.

Realization 4

    a. Defining ourselves by our history holds on to toxins, because the obsolete of yesterday lived today is toxic to a conscious life.

    b. The denser the body is, the quicker it ages, because the more it is at variance with the fluid unfolding of Cosmic Life.

    c. The past is to be viewed as a story or series of stories. A good play or movie can influence our perception and emotions just like art, but it does not cause us to identify with it – it is unreal.

Visualization 4

Look over your life's memories by scanning them with detachment, the way you would look at a movie script. Group parts of your life into separate categories such as:

- Birth to 6 years old
- 6-12 years old
- 12-18 years old
- and so forth …

If there are parts of a category you do not like, either change it or cut it out all together. When you are happy with it, bind it into a book and visualize a name for it on the cover. Place the books on a shelf.

Realization 5

    a. The more we empty the mind of memory, the more instant recall we have when we need it. Instant recall produces a photographic 'memory' that comes only as needed.

    b. All can be known when it needs to be. Looking back prevents us from experiencing even greater things now.

    c. Genius is the effortless knowing of an empty mind. It does not drain resources needed for the continual rejuvenation of the bodily field.

    d. The body only needs rejuvenation when it still lives in identity. When it surrenders fully to the vastness of existence, it is incorruptible.

Visualization 5

- Envision, like an overview, the life of duties and responsibilities that you live. Scan it briefly.
- Envision yourself alone, camping by a lake. You are content – eating fruit, nuts, and berries – having all you need. Feel the silence. Drop all masks, even the ones that you wear for yourself. Keep doing this envisioning until a peace of no expectations, no agendas, and no duties fills you entirely. Do this thoroughly.
- Envision your other life of duties again. Scan it briefly, like a speeded up movie.
- Envision yourself camping again. Do this until peace fills you …

Realization 6

The natural you without the masks is the real 'child of eternity.' The other life in the matrix is but a stage play.

HOW TO REMOVE THE TALONS OF TENSION CAUSED BY LINEAR TIME

Tension in the body comes from linear time, which is caused by resistance to life. Make 'time-slots' in your life in which you do nothing but unhook from doingess and experience beingness.[13] You will not be meditating, listening to music, watching television or reading. All outside communication will be turned off, like computers, phones, etc.

Stock up on food if you intend to do this for a weekend or longer (even ½ hour a day is helpful) so that you do not need to interact with others.

Sleep when you are tired and eat when you are hungry. Use candlelight as much as possible. If thoughts arise, do not engage them. Cover your mirrors, if you are doing this for days. Do not look into a mirror if you are only able to do it for an hour or so.

If tension persists anywhere in the body, blow out the tension with deep breaths. Envision yourself blowing out the tension from that area. When areas of the body resist life, they leak resources.

---

13 Eventually they blend into one as you become familiar with both equally.

The Labyrinth of Renewal

Kia-Shatach Saradesi

Ravenous for the black waters of life, which can only be drawn with the voice, many speak but say nothing ...

To speak from the shallow cup of the little self, depletes our supply. To communicate from the well-spring of existence feeds immortality ...

THE MEDITATION OF YOUTHENING

"With rage have we pounded with verbal onslaughts against the prison bars of our voice. In our self-made cells, from belief systems forged, have we sought our awaited release ..."

Place yourself into a deep, meditational state of complete relaxation. Breathe out all stress in any area of the body until all tension has dissolved.

Realization 1

- For most, the voice is the primary form of expression for the little egoic self, the egoic self that thinks itself to be the individual body, feelings and thoughts.
- Anything expressing from separation consciousness depletes the limited resources of the body, causing aging, decay and poor health.
- Every time you speak, it is causing aging, yet most fritter their resources away by filling the silences they fear with idle chatter.

Visualization 1

A deer of light, a spirit deer, grazes in peace in the meadow. A movement of the tall grass, then another, spreads like a rippling ring around the deer. Like an army of one, wild dogs take up their positions for the kill.

Ravenous, seething with ancient rage, they gather to take their revenge on the light. Silent is the tribe, united in anger, screaming strident communications through their hair. The wild dogs close in to slake their thirst for the blood of another's light ...

Realization 2

- As opposite poles of each other, light and frequency are in opposition to each other – the one thrives at the other's expense.
- During ascension cycles, light dominates and noise and voices representing frequency become obsessively strident – seeking to be heard.
- We have been in a light-based ascension for many years. The feminine has become suppressed and has seethed against the masculine dominance.
- To compensate for its having been reduced, the feminine unites as a tribe, its causes enforced by verbal communication.
- We confirm the uniformity of our belief systems with words. The words form an increasingly thick maze around us.

Visualization 2

The Song of the Wild Dogs[14]

Our growls unravel your connections
Unspin your mazes of belief
We seek to eat, in raw, live dying power
That which we are not …

Without this, we do not exist
The power of our collective jaw
Masticates light
Forces of unity binds our tribe

Realization 3

- Speaking without the deep desire to communicate is an act of aggression and defiance against life, for it is an attempt to control through words.

---

14 Received by Alicia.

- We see through our skin and hear with our whole body. Why then must we speak from the shallow vehicle of our throat alone? It is not so – we are meant to speak through our hair; through every follicle of our body.
- Does this not affirm the arrogance of the little self; thinking it can control the mighty river of life? Not if we speak with the voice of the Infinite.

Pull from the Black Moon well, deep within
Now, use your voice to weave potentialized,
sacred water into your skin.

- The voice that comes from the will drains the individual's meager supply. Opening the gate of living water in the throat pours through us the potential creation of perfection that becomes a reality as we speak it. Our words become alive and bring our environmental creations alive.

Feed this supply to your roots
Concentrate and don't spill
The Alchemy of Voice and Truth
Recalibrates that of Will.

Visualization 3

A dark, black river, like liquid night, pours from the depth of your throat, through your mouth in a directed flow. The flow washes away all old mediocrity that stands like rigid ruins along the way. It shapes new fluid forms that fulfill the hopes of your heart. It fills your body and washes away the black road of past memories. It is precious – the substance of life, it is not to be spilled or wasted with idle talk and attempts to placate and pander.

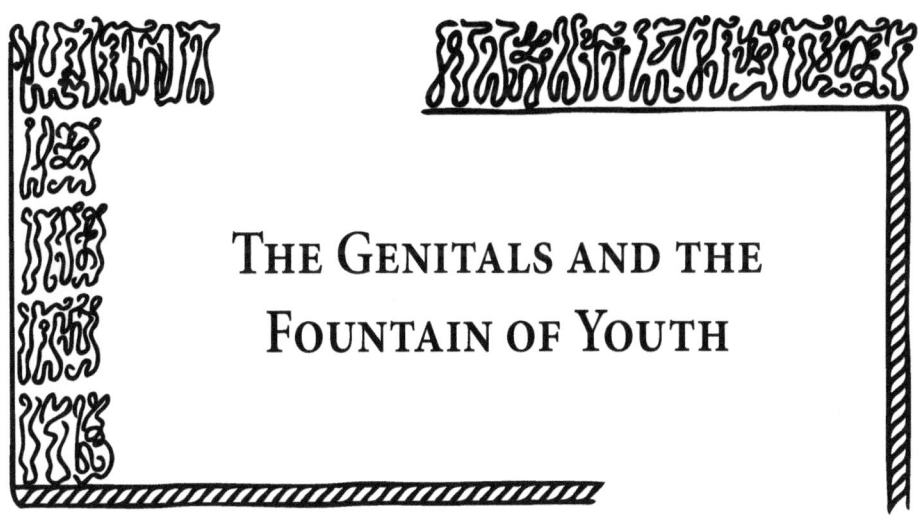

The Genitals and the Fountain of Youth

*Many have sought the fountain of youth.
Look to the genitals, the fountain of life
Transcending self-gratification
Their higher function of divinity awaits ...*

Almine

The Meditation of the Fountain of Youth

What is the moment, but a dot on a line?
Small as it is, it is still linear time ...

The genitals were made to birth the moment, conceived by memory that is moved and shaped by human hopes. Like a golden rope of two strands entwined, memory is rigid – a maze formed by the past, of hopes and dreams that do not flow fluidly from the heart and do not with the past combine – shaping a rigid moment.

The higher function of the genitals is to birth moments of higher and higher consciousness. This enables increasingly higher abilities to express divine potential. When hopes and dreams are flowing through and release the rigid memories of the past, the present is not bound by the past.

Now you receive a gold knotted rope
One part Divine, one part human hope
You must engage its connection fluidly between the two
For at all times this connection will unveil the divine in you.

Alicia

The Genitals are the Birthplace of the Moment

The testicles of a male and the vulvae of a female serve the same function: as antennae of the masculine and feminine components of the past.

1. The masculine components of the past, the rigid beliefs and memories that form mazes, are mind-based.
2. The feminine components of the past – the hopes and dreams of the feminine, heart-based components of the past – were meant to affect the masculine by creating desired changes. It was to become fluid structure.

When polarity became very accentuated, the feminine became so suppressed that it lost its hopes. The moment's creations became static. The left vulva or testicle, which is feminine and had to receive the hopes of the past, became dormant. Only the right one received the static past and perpetuated it in the moment.

The penis or vagina is the birthplace of the moment and determines the quality and creativity of the moment. If conception is based on polarity, masculine and feminine input, it perpetuates illusion and drains the resources available – hence it causes aging. The dysfunction present in the left testicle or vulva has leaked a great deal of energy.

The key to remedy the genitals causing aging to occur lies in two steps:

1. The left vulva and testicle must be brought to their full capacity and highest level of functionality.
2. The vulvae and testicles must become androgynous, in being equally receptive and pro-active.

The above steps are done by using sound.

METHOD

Sit on the floor with your legs and hands crossed; the right hand is holding the left knee and the left hand is holding the right knee.

1. Take a deep breath and with your mouth forming a small circle, make a long 'ooooh' sound as follows:
   - Start as high in pitch as you can possibly tone and make a descending 'ooooh' sound (as you slowly release the breath) to as low as you can possibly tone.
   - Take a deep breath and starting in as low a pitch as possible, ascend with the 'ooooh' sound to as high a pitch as you can possibly tone while slowly releasing the breath.

2. Repeat the ascending and descending 'ooooh' sounds four times each.
3. Remain in the same seated position.
4. Repeat steps 1 and 2 using the 'aaaah' sound.
5. Repeat steps 1 and 2 using the 'hmmm' sound.

We come in Androgyny

Hum your music the same ...

Pass sexuality, release the Reign

Translations from a Lemurian Scroll

The dictators of life have been husband and wife;
the rigid flow of memories man holds.

No more illusion to dictate life's course,
open the door for guidance from Source ...

The womb slumbers, now let it awake
A small, hard womb in man can do the same
Like the womb, it is a holy gate
In men it is known as the prostate

When the womb is set free
So the bodily cells will be
The breath is the answer to open the gate
Limitless resources this will create

The Mystical Properties of the Vagina and Penis

The womb or prostate represents the Cosmos (created life contained in an embryonic sac – the Cosmic membrane).

The penis or vagina draws resources from the limited supply of the uterus/prostate to create the reality of the individual. This brings about depletion and decay on a micro-cosmic and macro-cosmic level.

This scenario is repeated over and over again in every cell. The cell itself draws resources from its own organelle, the component that produces cellular energy. Again, the depletion brings about a limited life-span and the decay associated with it.

To transcend mortality, a limitless supply of resources must be found; only the Real is limitless.

MEDITATION TO RESTORE THE MYSTICAL ABILITIES

Place yourself into a meditative state. Breathe out all tension until the body feels totally relaxed.

Realization 1

Trauma, shame and blame create blockages and programs in the resources that are meant to flow from the uterus/prostate through the vagina/penis to create a reality from our hopes and dreams.

Anything that desires to transcend from one level to the next must first be brought into balance, with healing and appreciation, before it can rise above its present condition.

For a system of limitation (which represents an incubation stage in the development of life) to yield to limitlessness, a pre-requisite is that it must be fully functional.

Visualization 1

Envision your prostate or uterus filling with a bright, light-blue light. See the light flow through the vagina or penis, filling the shaft. See it flow through the shaft and 'out' into your environment.

See a desired reality starting to form from this light. Spend time envisioning the flow of the light, like a river, creating new excellence in your life.

Realization 2

Anything that aligns with the Infinite cannot draw from a finite supply of resources.

Old, rigid boundaries are eliminated by breath and sound. Frequency can destructure form.

Listen with your skin and lay your breath bare, set your cells free ...

Visualization 2

Lying flat on your back, see a ball of blue light at the bottom of your left foot. With an ascending 'aaaah' from a low to a high pitch, raise the ball of light up the left leg into the uterus/prostate.

Breathe out and tone 'ooooh' from a high pitch to a low one as the ball of light moves down the right leg to the bottom of the right foot.

Breathe the ball up the right leg with an ascending 'aaaah' sound into the uterus/prostate.

Breathe out with a descending 'ooooh' sound while moving the ball of light down the left leg into the foot.

Soundlessly, breath the ball up the left leg and hold it in the uterus/prostate for a few breaths while seeing it grow brighter and brighter.

Breathe in as deeply as possible and force the breath out as hard as you can through your mouth as the uterus or prostate 'explodes'. Force the breath out until a guttural sound emerges from your mouth and there is no more air left in your lungs ("... lay your breath bare").

Do this again and again; each time feeling your cells explode, losing all cellular boundaries ("set your cells free ...")

Now dissolve your bones, your back and your blood
Receive from the Universe ...

Keep working with the Voice

Move currents in harmony with Alchemy

Its an essential route to weaving your worlds and will

Reveal to you, the world you wish to be ...

Realization 3

No boundaries exist. There is no difference between you and your world in spacelessness. All that is, is yours to draw upon.

Visualization 3

Through your uterus/prostate (or the space where it etherically exists if it has been removed) a silver mist pours through and around your body at all times.

Create your hopes within this misty cocoon and expand it 'out' to the environment, knowing there is no out or in, just the boundless One Life, expressing as the many.

A silver cloaked Goddess will now walk with Thee ...

Bonus Section

The Illuminations of Eternal Life

*Among us they walk, god-beings in the flesh,
from forgotten beginnings, ancient ones are they ...*

The Atlantean Records of the Angels

Bonus Section: The Illuminations of Eternal Life

PROPHECY FROM ANGELS

Pelesh vaarash haravi pelesh heres tre va nuravi. Pra nich herstave nunushvi

Three books there are, a trilogy to come
The books of the gods of the Holy One

Peleh tre hersba nechvi: Sevech par avis tra u na sabis kelesh urasta prave

Join them together and holy water shall come,
Holy the wheels of the holy ones

Perech michva bilech mishpata trechve selveva nirechtu harasta milechp uvraset

Embody the truths, illuminations they are called,
A new way of perception begun by the few, given to all

Kunavish trechvar selvevit mistrehur unesve klehutrat

The magic of gods will be released
The capstone released
Doors open wide

INTRODUCTION TO THE GOD KINGDOM

The God kingdom is the apex of evolution for all races. The elf or angel or human, on every planet and on every level of existence, aspires to evolve into this kingdom. The Gods of existence form the cosmic government and because the Earth is the cradle of civilization, the greatest number of gods and goddesses are found here.

Gods are also created to fulfill certain mandates and to help govern specific portions of existence. Many secrets surround the kingdom of the gods but perhaps the one that fires the imagination the most is the fact that many gods and goddesses are embodied and among us today.

The opportunities for beings on Earth to evolve into godhood are readily available. The fact that the Earth has, since 2005, been the way-shower or pivot point of cosmic ascension has meant that it is the microcosmic pivot point for all life – a great service to render. Such a service is opening up access to accelerated evolution and blessings of consciousness. The diversity on Earth also provides beings with the ability to experience many different perspectives and learning opportunities. Its density has created intensity in the experiences of humanity. This too can accentuate rapid growth.

Information is available on how to reach advanced levels of existence and long-hidden tools have been released to aid man's journey. Alchemy, incorruptible white magic, Kaanish Belvaspata[15] and other mystical techniques are finally released to humanity to bestow their blessings. The angels have brought their most precious hidden mysteries, and the Toltec seers have released theirs. The rest is up to us.

Kiriras Agawavanti miruk helstat uheravasvi minuvash, isinat heretuk vasva

From the Infinite's throne, the Gods of Source come forth to share gifts of luminosity.

---

15 See *Belvaspata, Angel Healing, Volume I.*

PROPHECY OF THE GODS FROM THE LIBRARY OF THE WHITE HORSE

The 16th Plate | Part IV

Kee-eehana birak heras paret harestu
Among us they walk, but we know them not
They hide among the ordinary where none know to seek
Immortal they are and never death shall see
Some through time tunnels came to walk with man,
Others for thousands of years have lived on the land
Some in isolation watch over human affairs
Most reside among men, though none know they're there
They overcome illusions that man might see
This is why they assume infirmities
When these records, holy and pure,
Are once again read, they need no longer endure
Let them from this service be set free
Let the God kingdom arise in majesty

The 16th Plate | Part V

One hundred and forty-four gods of the throne
Carry in their hearts what they know alone
Each has a wheel, a most sacred tool
That tells of the Infinite's Holy rule

The birth of individuated life
The secrets within the wheels describes
The release of the secrets is only one part
Of what each god will release from the heart

The wheel itself activated becomes
When its corresponding secret is assimilated by one
Move then from the feet to the head, the wheels
As all hundred and forty-four have moved through, godhood is achieved

When a truth represented by a single wheel
Is not embodied, discomfort you'll feel
For stuck it shall be; as you try to move it through
Pressure this will create within you[16]

As the insights are embodied by you,
The purpose of Creation you'll do
For long ago when life began
The purpose of Creation became the destiny of man

---

16 Contemplate the insight until the wheel move freely through.

Bonus Section: The Illuminations of Eternal Life

The purpose fulfilled, the human kingdom you may forsake
For you, a greater destiny awaits
The God kingdom, a much higher evolutionary line begins
The transfiguration shall begin within

When the first hundred and forty-four creations were conceived
The Infinite did so in a dream
The hundred and forty-four purposes of life
Were embodied within, as unyielded light

A shadow was cast, illusion began
As the first race was created, the children, the man
The purposes were defined by what they could not be
By the shadows they cast, they were clearly seen

Now is the time the unyielded insights to release
That the shadows they cast may forever cease
That the occlusions within the gods' hearts
May be replaced with transparency and forever depart

ILLUMINATION TABLET No. 1

Bonus Section: The Illuminations of Eternal Life

THE EQUATION FOR 144 ILLUMINATIONS

[illegible glyphs] + [illegible glyphs] + [illegible glyphs] + [illegible glyphs] + [illegible glyphs]
+
[illegible glyphs] + [illegible glyphs] + [illegible glyphs] + [illegible glyphs] + [illegible glyphs]
+
[illegible glyphs] + [illegible glyphs] + [illegible glyphs] + [illegible glyphs] + [illegible glyphs]
+
[illegible glyphs] + [illegible glyphs] + [illegible glyphs] + [illegible glyphs] + [illegible glyphs]
+
[illegible glyphs] + [illegible glyphs] + [illegible glyphs] + [illegible glyphs] + [illegible glyphs]
+
[illegible glyphs] + [illegible glyphs] + [illegible glyphs] + [illegible glyphs] + [illegible glyphs]
+
[illegible glyphs] + [illegible glyphs] + [illegible glyphs] + [illegible glyphs] + [illegible glyphs]
+
[illegible glyphs] + [illegible glyphs] + [illegible glyphs] + [illegible glyphs] + [illegible glyphs]
+
[illegible glyphs] + [illegible glyphs] + [illegible glyphs] + [illegible glyphs] + [illegible glyphs]
+
[illegible glyphs] + [illegible glyphs] + [illegible glyphs] + [illegible glyphs] + [illegible glyphs]
+
[illegible glyphs] + [illegible glyphs] + [illegible glyphs] + [illegible glyphs] + [illegible glyphs]
+

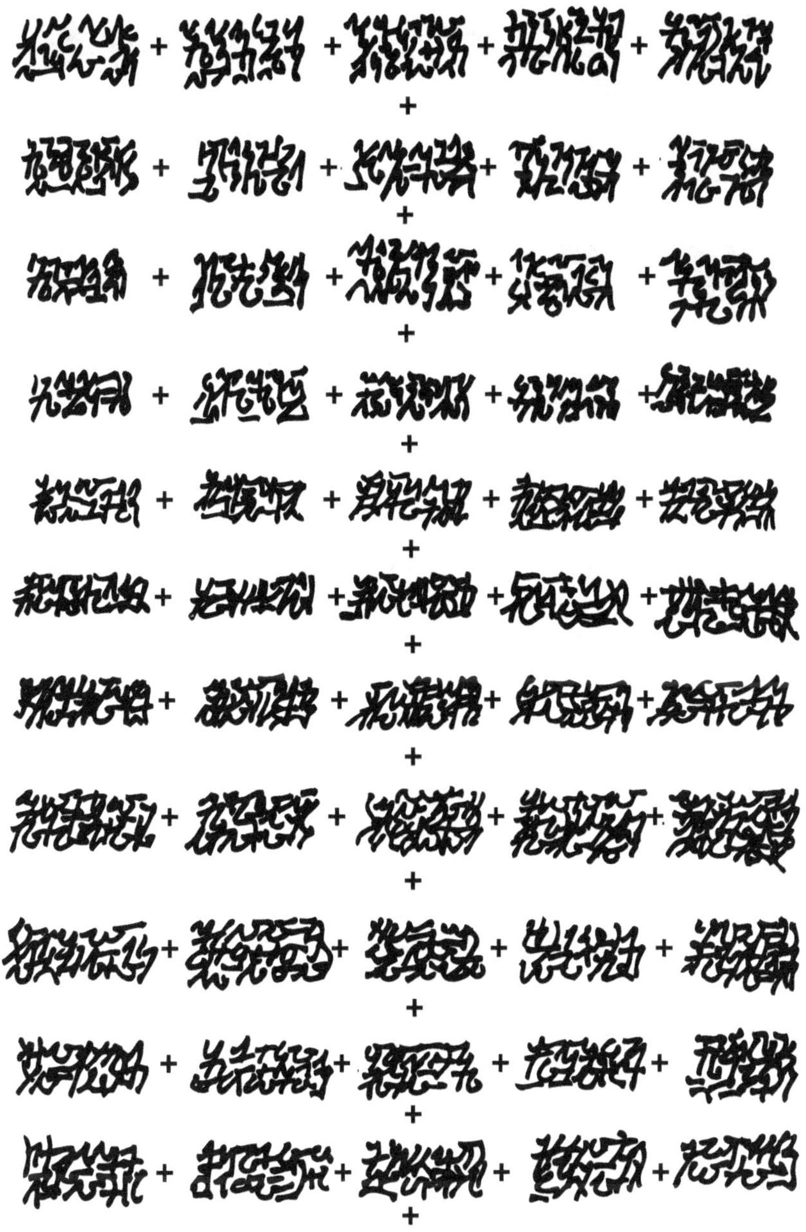

Bonus Section: The Illuminations of Eternal Life

Illuminations of the Gods

ILLUMINATION 1

Illusion comes from an absence of light. To find the source of illusion, seek the understanding that is missing.

Exploitation comes from a misplaced desire for order. The mind perceives order as the compartmentalizing of life, the separating of oneness for the purpose of controlling through definition.

True order is the never-ending spontaneous flow of perfection of the One Life. Compartmentalization is duality. The nature of mind has been separative, to try to map out the incomprehensible. Those that seek to exploit are acting out the need of mind to create boundaries, by forcing others to do so.

By illuminating the recognition of the oneness of life, the true inclusive nature of mind assumes its place on the thrones of our lives. We live the truth that there is no relationship, there is only One Life.

ILLUMINATION 2

Mind can only decide whether an action is worth taking based upon assessment of past experience. Time as linear is an illusion. The past does not exist as real; all there is, is the fluid eternal moment. Because life changes in an exponential way as the fluid moment flows, linear predictability of outcome is impossible.

The addiction of mind to 'know' prevents us from allowing the spontaneous explosion of life's possibilities, keeping us in bondage to the mediocrity of the past. Addiction arises from self-abandonment. Mind abandons its inner knowingness by trying to understand itself through looking for answers without.

The illusion of without and within space disappears when truth is illuminated. That which appears to be without is part of us as well; the only reason anything can speak to us is because it is us speaking to ourselves.

ILLUMINATION 3

The gullible tendency of man to blindly follow arises from an inner prompting to receive and comply with the will of the Infinite. Creation was made to express the Divine Intent, to listen to the promptings of the Infinite's unfolding of new potential for expression.

When the tyranny of mind replaced the soft whispers of the Divine, the deep-seated knowingness that free will is an illusion remained, leaving an information vacuum. This was a vulnerability that led us to take guidance from anyone who, with great conviction, could override our objections by convincing us that they know and we don't. The more sensitive we are, the more acutely we are aware that we don't know.

The illumination that life is an experience, not a set of guidelines to live by, needs to replace the need to know. Knowing consists of prison bars.

ILLUMINATION 4

Few are able to take responsibility for their own actions. Resources are expended without the guidance and understanding of the heart's motives. The creation of the illusion of intelligence, formed by mind to differentiate between the compartments it had created, contributes to this. Intelligence chooses between one thing and another. It labels one thing as good and another as less so, leading to the origin of value judgments, as well as those of guilt and innocence.

It is under the labels of guilt and innocence that the motives for our actions hide. The mind's labeling is not flexible. It stereotypes and imprisons just as surely as any jailer, and gaining freedom is not easily accomplished.

When life is the expression of the One and mind has merged into the inclusive eternal mind that embraces rather than divides, there is no guilt. There can be no guilt when there is no choice, for we have become blended with the Will of the Infinite.

ILLUMINATION 5

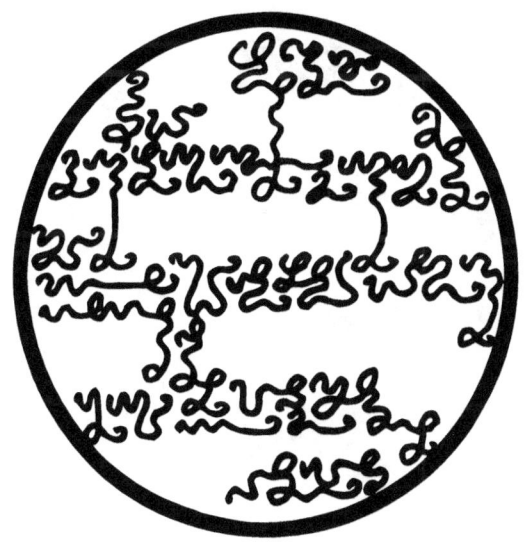

Heroism and martyrdom have been extolled within individuated life. They are nevertheless illusions. How can one part of the ocean sacrifice itself for another part of the ocean, when the ocean is indivisible and incorruptible? Even if it could be so, would taking from one part to give to another not change the whole?

And if heroism consists in taking bold action in the face of a perceived threat, let us examine this illusion also. The person in oneness and vision sees the highest choice at all times: that which most fully reflects who we are, the one vast being having a human experience. In seeing it, we have no choice. To live less than our highest vision is un-impeccable. It is said: 'Fortune favors the brave'. The reason for this is that all of life supports one who lives in his highest truth; one who knows he is all that is.

ILLUMINATION 6

Responsibility can be carried like an identity, designating someone as being able to be counted on. The arrogance of thinking that we are needed in the ever-changing fluid patterns of life – that the smooth unfolding of life around us depends upon our contribution – is a fallacy.

We do what is placed before us in the moment, with a great sense of adventure, for it is the doorway to the unfolding of life. When confronted with a choice, we gauge its validity by the joy it may bring, confident in the fact that our selection is already known and that life has already conformed around the outcome in a pattern of perfection.

We are not responsible for carrying life. Instead, it is cradling us in a cherished embrace.

ILLUMINATION 7

The inclination to be a 'respecter' of people, to value one above another, is a remnant of the value judgments of intelligence created by separative mind. This illusion has held the masterful life of grace hostage and personal empowerment in a stranglehold. Few are exempt from its clutches.

There is a flawed premise that if one has a child, it is to be expected that one would love that child more than other children. This depends upon how 'more' is defined. If it means that the degree to which other children are loved is less, we do not see the One Life running through all children. If it means there are more opportunities to see the wonder of life through the child you can watch grow from birth to adulthood, it is simply like looking through one window rather than another.

ILLUMINATION 8

Much effort is expended endeavoring to change our perspective to a higher one, to raise our perception. When all things are known to us and it is simply a matter of accessing such information, to what are we raising our perspective? There are no such things as accidents, nor is there anything in the cosmos to fix. If there is an 'occlusion' on any given moment in our perception, it is to guide us in a direction of Infinite intent, like a pathway that becomes illuminated by dimming the surrounding forest.

The highest or best perception we can have for guidance in any moment is exactly the one we have. If there are portions of our vision dimmed, it is so the path can be more clearly indicated. This applies to others as well. We should remember this, as they make choices that appear flawed to us. There are no flawed choices. There is only the path along which we are led to perfection.

ILLUMINATION 9

Humor does not belong only to humankind. If we could understand, we could see that animals laugh too. Crows play pranks on one another. Animals and plants laugh when tickled by bees. Yet the accessing of the holy is viewed as a solemn affair – laughter at such times viewed as inappropriate. Self-appointed spiritual leaders put on solemn faces to indicate how much in touch with the Divine they are.

Cosmic bliss is the movement of the Being of the Infinite. When a person experiences bliss, it is because to some extent the movement of the Infinite is felt within the cells – something more easily available when the cellular nucleus enlarges during mastery.

Humor is the holy experience of momentarily entering into the bliss of cosmic movement. Laughter is the release of such an overwhelmingly large experience. We enter the holy of holies through humor and it leaves us euphoric.

ILLUMINATION 10

Many have sought to remove density within life, wanting all to be illuminated. Great patterns of moving light of various gradations dance spontaneously within existence. Changing areas of existence through varying shades of light is an exuberant expression of the Infinite's joy in beingness.

Density is nothing more than the areas of light that are slightly dimmed, without which there can be no pattern. It is the note that is not played as it waits its turn to add to the exquisite symphony of life. If all notes are played at once, there can be no music. If all light shines equally bright, there can be no definitions and no pattern.

Density, if it means that which does not belong, does not exist. If it means the deliberate withholding of the starburst of light each being is, so that they may contribute to the perfection of life unfolding, it does and should exist.

ILLUMINATION 11

Authority is a structure of illusion, based on the self-appointed authority of mind. Authority in the form of external government cannot exist because relationship, the premise upon which it is based, does not exist. In accepting it or imposing it as real, we validate the unreal.

The only real government there is, is the self-government of the individual. The question may then be asked, if there is no freedom of choice, as we are enticed by our level of perception to participate in the cosmic dance, what we are governing?

We have the opportunity to gain insights into the self from the experience life leads us to. When we do, we contribute to the intricacy of the pattern of life, helping to shape the beauty of the dance. We are not needed to accomplish this, but rather are given the opportunity to share the joy.

ILLUMINATION 12

There is no real standard for beauty. The stem of the flower is not expected to appear as the bloom, nor the roots that languish in the cool depths of the soil to be like the leaves.

What makes the stem beautiful is the perfection with which it fulfills the purpose of its creation; the firmness with which it lifts the flower unto the sun; the pliant resilience with which it bends in the storm. Each being has a specific part to play in the Being of the One Life.

Each is uniquely beautiful in that beauty matches function. Yet none are locked into a specific function and should life call for us to flow in another direction, we may. The aged may youthen and the care-worn become filled with lightness of being, yet the aged have no less beauty than the young.

ILLUMINATION 13

Conflict has existed among beings since the onset of individuated life. Yet in reality, there cannot be conflict. Because of this, there cannot be solutions either. What there can be is creative flow.

If the wild river, flowing freely and spontaneously, did not have its ever-altering obstacle course, its very nature would be compromised. It would no longer be a river, but a predictable canal. It is the newly fallen tree that alters the river's course that provides the spontaneous change in its shape.

Let us embrace the illumination that no two beings exist. All lives within us as part of the eternal symphony, orchestrated by the Infinite.

ILLUMINATION 14

Empathically resonating with the hardship of others can be an added perceived burden for those who are sensitive. When a note is played on a piano, careful observation will show every similar note in every octave vibrating in empathic resonance.

We only empathically resonate with what is already within our own lives, else we would not recognize, nor take on the emotions of another. The empath is therefore more sensitive than most in seeing the areas where illusion lingers within their own perception causing distortion of emotion.

This too is in perfection. But when someone before us strikes a discordant note that resonates within us, it is time to move beyond it. We are not picking up someone else's debris – there is only one being: oneself.

ILLUMINATION 15

In the moment, we contain all that is. Overwhelm cannot exist because in the moment, infinite resources are accessed. It is when our workload is assessed linearly that we try to carry the accomplishments of many moments in the moment of the now. It is when work is seen in chunks that we cut ourselves off from cosmic resources and the load becomes heavy.

Are we overwhelmed by the grandeur of our vision, of eternal joy flowing through our hearts? The outlets for such strong feelings that threaten to engulf us are laughter, song, tears, physical exercise or dance. The grandeur of the Infinite feels overwhelming only when we see ourselves as separate from It. The truth is that we are to dissolve ourselves into and become one with It.

ILLUMINATION 16

Power is released when a lower order changes to a higher order. For either order to exist implies that there are moments when the exuberant flow of Infinite life is contained and static, that a matrix can in reality exist and that life is less than spontaneous.

Power is not only the effect of change but seen as necessary to effect change. What could we possibly want to change if all beings are acting, not of their volition, but as part of the orchestrated perfection of the whole? If opposition is merely a signal from the One Life to change direction, how can it be seen as something to remove? In a cosmos of perfection, there is nothing to change; there is nothing for which power is needed. The One Life supports us.

ILLUMINATION 17

Comparison implies relationship and attempts to define something by what it is not. This type of definition mistakenly leads us to believe that we understand the essence of something because we can see what it is not. Yet this reveals nothing of what it is.

If comparison is done to determine value, we are using the old illusory tool of intelligence and imposing non-existent, past experiential knowledge and value systems on the newness of the moment.

There are times when the tiny tack is needed. There are times when the big bolt is exactly right. Each is perfect for a unique function.

There is no way we can determine value other than by what is applicable for this moment. Choices can only be deemed as accurate or not, moment by moment, as life dances on its way.

ILLUMINATION 18

Energy is the result of the movement of something between two parts, or the dispersal of energy – the result of movement away from a point of origin.

If we had freedom of choice, we would be in a separate space within the Infinite's Being. We would also be artificial intelligence and unreal. But as part of the limitless Being of One Life, we are real and no longer have a separate movement from the whole. We move as the Infinite moves, in limitless Oneness.

We have become directionless movement without points of origin or reference points. Like the ocean, we have become all resources and they no longer exist separate from us. Energy has no real existence.

ILLUMINATION 19

Life-force has been defined as that which enlivens. It is inherent within the creation of the Infinite, rather than the artificial sub-creations of man. It is one of the building blocks of existence and, like all others, an illusion.

Does the table or the chair man has made truly exist? No, for within the One Life only one Self-Creator exists. In fluidity, the Infinite self-creates moment by moment. There is no place for rigid structure and, as man sees through the illusions, the sub-creations will begin to disappear. The physical body will fluidly change moment by moment as we do. In spaceless space it is a fluid part of the dance, no longer a rigid reference point in the vastness of our Being.

ILLUMINATION 20

Life affirming joyousness of the Self is the quality of the true reality of life. There is no possibility that self-destructiveness can exist. Life dances in joyous innovation. There is no place for structure.

Attempts to create controlled structure bring stagnation, decay and self-destructiveness. These things are illusions.

When mind created structures, it also invented the concept that growth was necessary. This replaced the illusion of destructiveness with the illusion of the need to strive in order to grow. As programs to strive kept us from being self-destructive, we became trapped in their illusions and others, like linear becoming. There is only life spontaneously lived.

ILLUMINATION 21

Indulging an illusion as part of personality, or by letting it become an identity, retains the illusion that we have that personality or identity. Personality either forms as a result of personal history or as a partial expression of all the traits of the One Life within us. In reality, there is no past, no memory of personal history. Everything lives within us and can be expressed. Illusion bars us from full expression and illusion cannot exist within the One Life.

It is not 'holy' or 'enlightened' to cling to separation-based views. That does not serve life. Let all fractures be gone – let wholeness reign.

ILLUMINATION 22

We have used suffering to stay contracted when we have encountered the limitless vastness of our being. Focusing on suffering allows us to avoid seeing our true self.

Suffering is an illusion born of the illusion that loss can occur, that we can be alone, that imperfection or injustice can exist within the perfection of The One Being. We allow this even as the fullness of life moves through us.

But within the vastness of life, neither contraction nor expansion can exist because there is no direction, nor is there a focal point. We are all things, filling the vastness of existence with our unique presence.

ILLUMINATION 23

Seeing flaws in others occurs when we do not want to see the same flaw in our self. The judgment is inflexible once intelligence pronounces it. The self-censure this brings is painful because of the misplaced trust we have given to the self-appointed authority of the intellect. If we are irrevocably branded as bad or flawed, we believe we do not deserve good things in life.

The missing perception is that creations of the Infinite cannot be flawed. All beings play roles that form the kaleidoscope of changing life within the One Being. All are therefore innocent participants in the joyous pageantry of existence.

ILLUMINATION 24

It is easier to see the support of the tribe than the support of the Oneness of Life. However, the individual cannot trust the illusion of relationship – in this case with the tribe – for support. The only support there is, is the self-support of the One Life.

The tribe traps with demands of conformity. It demands that the individual behave according to the tribe's ideas of what is normal; that bright lights be dimmed in exchange for the sense of false security which the tribe offers.

Instead we must adopt the absolute conviction that our being is our sustenance and that the One Life, of which we are an integral part, is our passage to freedom from ensnarement by the tribe's illusory promises of acceptance and support.

ILLUMINATION 25

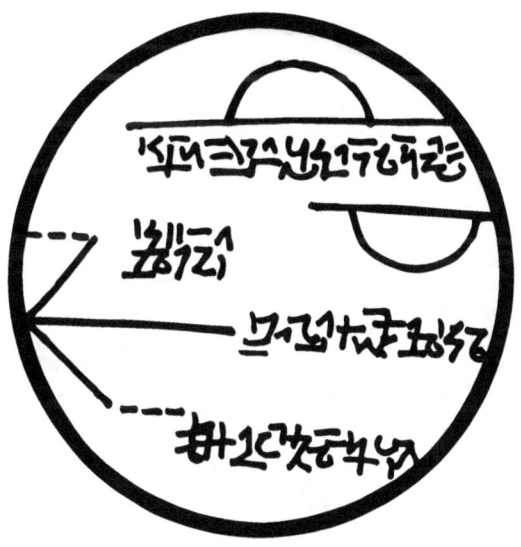

Disillusionment and disappointment when our ideals are not met and life around us seems much more unenlightened than we are, weighs heavily on the shoulders of lightworkers. Life seems inhospitable to the bright lights of the world.

The definition of the bright lights comes from the fact that the surrounding lights are dimmer. Every concerto has it crescendos and every dance it apex. Because we happen to be the apex of our surroundings does not mean the dance itself is mediocre, or that others may not yet surpass our brightness. Only the Grand Choreographer spontaneously delegates the roles.

ILLUMINATION 26

Complexity and simplicity cannot be viewed as having their own individual realities. They are indivisibly connected, like two sides of one coin. As the cosmic symphony is playing, we can isolate and hear only the sound of the one note, middle C, as it is played every few bars. We would call this selective hearing of the one note 'simplicity'.

Alternatively, we could call the whole symphony complex, yet it is made up of single notes. In this way simplicity and complexity are both the result of an error of perception or hearing. The whole is a spontaneous production that defies description as it changes each part of the fluid, eternal moment.

ILLUMINATION 27

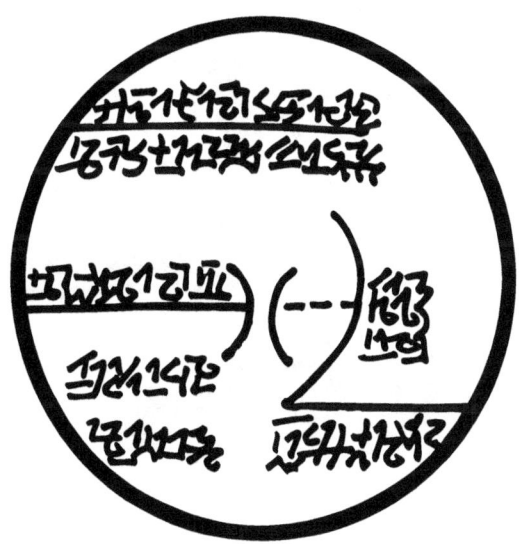

Life seems to require so much of us. Yet the only valid requirement is that we surrender to the One Life in which we exist, that we trust the benevolent support of That which gave us life. We were not created to suffer. Suffering is after all, only an illusion. We were created to revel in the joy of living.

The self-imposed burdens of life have come through allowing the social conditioning and programs of others to govern us. When it is realized that we have forever as a being of immortality, the haste to accomplish certain things within a certain time frame ceases. We lay our burdens down and enjoy our work as part of the adventure.

ILLUMINATION 28

Expectations of duration are formed by the bondage of linear time. We assume from past experience that traveling or task or sleep require certain amounts of time. Because of our expectations, this illusion is perpetuated.

When we live in the timelessness of the One Life, the illusion of electro-magnetics, which is part of duality, does not exist. It has been this illusion that has given the appearance of a delay between cause and effect. Eliminating clocks as much as we can, together with our flawed expectations of linear time, will set us free.

ILLUMINATION 29

We regard some people as fortunate and others as unfortunate. This illusion fails to recognize that every life is perfect within the grand design. A second illusion is that ease of living, as we perceive it, brings more joy or more fulfillment than a more arduous life.

We so often do not see the pain of a fruitless life or one devoid of love and passion. The stress felt by a CEO driving an expensive car is less obvious than that of the person who must catch a fish for his next meal. In truth, the life of the latter may be far more satisfying, tranquil and life-enhancing.

ILLUMINATION 30

Categorizing as holy and unholy or proper and improper comes from the judgments of the intellect. Using past conditioning as a gauge, it attempts to control through labeling. Trying to fit our lives into categories diminishes more and more the spontaneity of our actions.

Those who live spontaneously, who are deemed 'wild and free' rather than 'civilized and responsible' are viewed with suspicion. The labeling is simply another form of programming by the tribe. The demeanor of those living freely and spontaneously could become contagious and control by the tribe could slip away. Man could instead break free into his natural state.

ILLUMINATION 31

Maturity is prized as a trait of leadership. Both these terms need to be examined for the illusions they are. Maturity carries the baggage of past programming and experiential knowledge. This closes the future to its new possibilities and denies the present its boundless exponential growth.

Because of the tendency of beings to follow authority, others are led around and around the fish bowl of the known in mediocrity. Leadership comes from certainty and conviction that the answers we have are valid. In every moment, the One Life changes all previous possibilities. There is absolutely no valid basis for predictability – the hallmark of mediocrity.

ILLUMINATION 32

Damage from trauma is an illusion based on the seeming belief that fracturing can occur; that anything can be made unwhole. This is compounded when the illusion of duration is applied – the belief that a certain amount of time is required to regain wholeness.

There is no ability to divide the ocean. The fracturing of the Infinite is an illusion. We are a consciousness superimposed over all that is and it is equally impossible to damage us. Neither wear and tear, in the form of aging, nor damage of any kind can in reality touch us as part of the incorruptible One Life.

ILLUMINATION 33

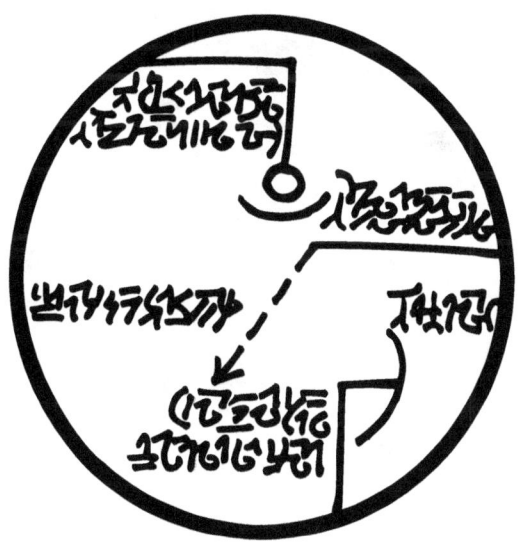

In reality, neither punishment nor restitution can exist, for they imply guilt and victimhood – illusory concepts that have no place in the perfection of the One Life.

Where life is continually renewed and eternally incorruptible, there is no need of paltry attempts to restore its balance or equalize the scores. We are not needed by the One Life in any way to maintain its perfection.

Nothing can be taken from one part of the ocean and given to another. Life itself will, like the ocean, immediately even the score.

ILLUMINATION 34

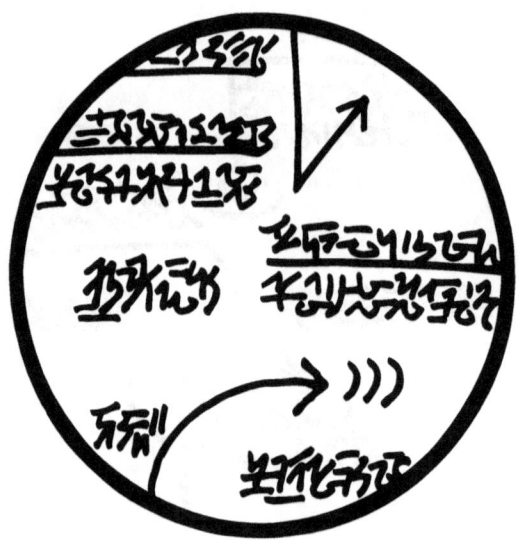

The body has served as a focal point so that we do not have to examine our own vastness. In this, we have abandoned ourselves. The abandoning of self invariably leads to addiction. Our bodily needs have become an addiction, screaming for our attention.

In the vastness of the One Life, the illusion of the body cannot exist; there can be no reference points for us to focus on. We therefore in reality have no dense bodies to keep our focus. One area of the ocean can be no more dense than another. Bodies are merely an image of fluid structure within our true vastness as the One Life.

ILLUMINATION 35

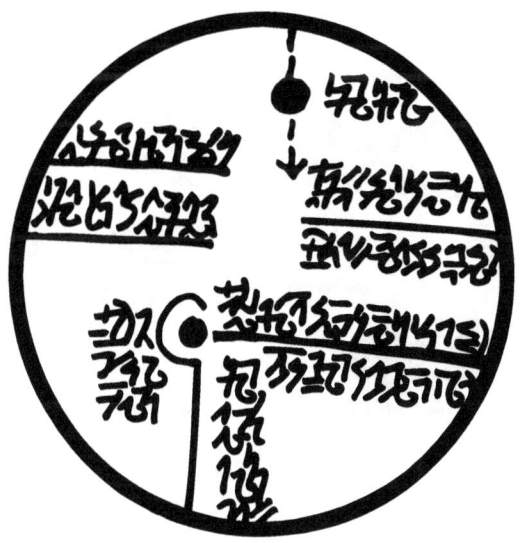

Awareness was part of the illusory building blocks of life while we existed within the matrix of the dream. It has been like the priest, a self-appointed intermediary to the Infinite. It is no longer an illusion that serves a purpose.

We have awakened to our true heritage to find we are all that is. As such, we are at all times directly in touch with all things. Awareness of a flower at the expense of the rest of life is a form of contraction or focus, creating separation and space – the part of existence we are aware of and the part we are not. This is an illusion, for all things are within us.

ILLUMINATION 36

The illusion of family comes from the need to belong and from the bonding ceremony of birth, and the romanticized outlook we have of birth, motherhood and fatherhood.

Wherever individuated life has a component of life that does not have an actual counterpart in the One Life, it is a sub-creation – a creation of the dream. We are not the Infinite's children, but creations that have become internalized components of the One Life. Birth only takes place because some still cling to the illusion of death even though all consists of immortal essence.

The need to belong can only exist in the absence of the unwavering vision that we are all that is.

ILLUMINATION 37

Sexuality as a need presupposes the illusion of relationship and, in most cases, gender. The fullness that exists within androgynous beings, knowing themselves to be all things, does not require sexuality with another to validate either his or her sexuality or to fulfill what some have perceived as self-lack.

To constantly exist from the fullness of one's being is an orgasmic and intimate love affair with the profound nuances of the diversity of all life forms. The dance of life is a consuming sensual interaction with self. The union with another is but a further expression of the same.

ILLUMINATION 38

Using currency to obtain sustenance and what we perceive to be the necessities of life is a sub-creation of man. It implies that an external illusion is the source of supply. The need to supply the body with external sustenance is in and of itself an illusion.

Our being is and always has been our source of limitless supply. We are heirs to the One Life's supply – wealthy beyond our wildest dreams. Accentuating this all-abundance through living and acknowledgment increases its presence within the wonder of our lives.

ILLUMINATION 39

Interpersonal love is preceded by what we think we know about someone. It is the preconceived information about that person that generates their lovability in our perception. Yet it is not possible to know anything about anyone, including oneself. As a perspective of the boundless whole, we are firstly too vast to comprehend and secondly, we are constantly experiencing the momentous changes of life's symphony moving through us.

Love and light have been the interconnected building blocks of life within the dream. Light, as the old wisdom teachings of the past, is dissolved – its obsolete teachings gone. So is its matching component love in its old form as the desire to include.

ILLUMINATION 40

Perception is the multi-sensory observing of a specific part of creation and, like awareness, contracts its focus to the exclusion of all else – an impossibility. Life is not divided into parts. There is not really an apple on the table to your right, or a flower on your left. You, the flower and the apple, having real life, are all inter-related and merged fields, inseparably connected. What appears as separated is merely a peculiarity of vision, the impression of separation and form. The apple or flower can be experienced within you, but not truly and in reality perceived.

Self-perception is likewise an impossibility. There is no vantage point from which to perceive yourself, since you are all things.

ILLUMINATION 41

The illusion that transitions are needed cannot be sustained when one considers that life is new every moment. There is no plan in place connected with a timetable requiring interim steps. There is no linear becoming that requires a gradual unfolding.

Life can be one way one moment and an entirely different way the next. There are no memories in place, because there is no such thing as electro-magnetic fields that hold and interpret memory. Memory has been held in the building blocks of life – all of which have been an illusion. None of them have ever really existed. All does change, every moment.

ILLUMINATION 42

The illusion of will must now disappear. No one can impose his or her will on life. Like freedom of choice, it does not exist. We mistakenly think that when confronted with choice, we have volition. Instead, our perception guides us to the right choice so that we stay in step with the dance of life.

We cannot impose will when we do not have the freedom of choice. The imposition of will is a form of control that we exercise to reach desired outcomes. The Infinite Itself does not have desired outcomes, but rather spontaneously expresses. The illusion of matrices and informational grids arises from the incorrect belief that our will can in any way affect life – blended with the One, we respond to The Conductor.

ILLUMINATION 43

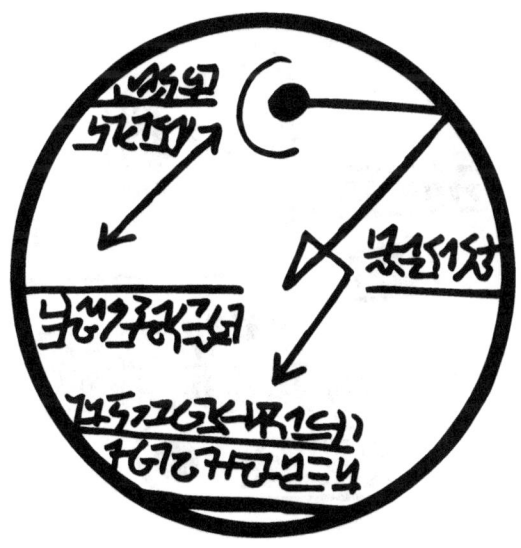

The illusion of sub-atomic particles, or that atomic elements exist, has kept their illusional function in place. It has affected our ability to differentiate the real from the unreal. That which is created by the Infinite – for example, an angel – is real. Yet our sensory perception and the mechanisms of interpretations have labeled it as unreal – the fault of the illusion of atomic and subatomic particles. The chair, a sub-creation of man, is not really there. Yet the illusion has been perpetuated.

The dissolving of the illusion of subatomic particles will allow us to know life directly for what it is.

ILLUMINATION 44

No roles exist as realities. Play no roles. Indulge no illusion. As a parent, you are indulging an illusion by playing a role, for are you not also a child? As a student, are you not also a teacher?

In former unenlightened shamanic practices, the practitioner would shape-shift to the band of the beast (the realities of animals) by moving what used to be the assemblage point downwards.

Now, by realizing that there are no forms or subatomic elements, we can see that the body of the wolf is as unreal as ours. We can manifest any form or forms at will, knowing they are not really there.

ILLUMINATION 45

It is time to let go the illusion of habits. How can a habit exist when memory does not? When neither past nor patterns exist, habits are robbed of the elements from which they are formed. Habits are like illusory banks of a river that pre-determine the river's flow. They stifle the imaginative and spontaneous expression of our lives with the illusion of their rigidness.

They form programs that determine our actions and provide the false sense of security that derives from the illusion of predictability. They create the illusion of a personal matrix – impossible within the spontaneous and glorious dance of the One Life.

ILLUMINATION 46

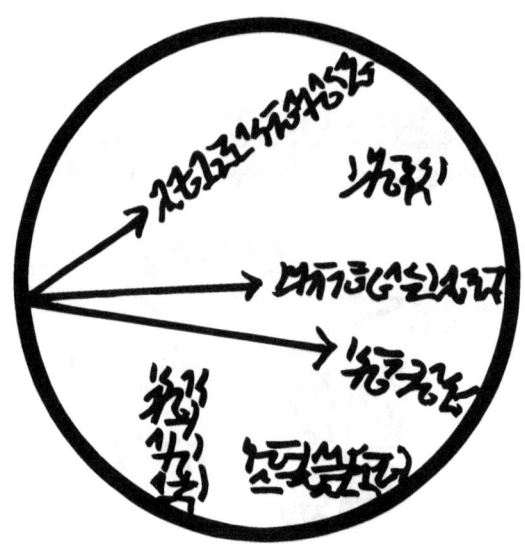

The great illusion is that the moment exists. Illusions rely on externals to define them. They exist by virtue of what they are not. An example of this would be space. It is defined by that which occupies it, that which it is not.

The same is true for the illusion of the existence of a moment. The moment exists because it is not the moment that went before, nor the one after. And although it says it is eliminating linear time, it causes it. It is a form of contracted vision and contraction is also an illusion within the One Being.

Life in no-time sets us free from the tyranny of form and of having to be in one place at one 'time'.

ILLUMINATION 47

There can be no definitions within the ever-renewing, spontaneously expressing Being of the One life. Nothing we have known within the Dream of existence can serve as a reference point to help determine the unfathomable vastness of the One Life.

Wisdom, knowledge and vocabulary fail in attempting to define or describe a life blended in the dance of formlessness of the One Life. Words define. Words are therefore mere illusions that strengthen the illusion of relationship and of thinking that we know. We must dissolve the illusion of thinking that words convey meaning in favor of the discovery unfolding throughout our being as part of the One Life.

Bonus Section: The Illuminations of Eternal Life

ILLUMINATION 48

Self-expression cannot be when the self does not exist if there is only One Being in existence. We are within the One Life like the various instrumental sections of the orchestra. The violin and drum sections do not play independent of the horns and reeds. The composer and conductor are responsible for directing all musical parts into a congruent whole.

The Divine Composer does not work from a score. The whole orchestral symphony is being composed as we go. The conductor's role is to encourage the correct interpretation of the music appearing on the screen before us. We have to play the correct notes, but ignoring the interpretation of the conductor is a choice.

ILLUMINATION 49

We have no real personal choice other than the quality of the moment – how well we live it, how much we see it and how much we enjoy it.

But surely, one might ask, if four dishes are placed on the table in front of us, we have the right to choose one? The choice we will ultimately make is determined by our particular perception level, cognitively or non-cognitively. This in turn is programmed by the One Life, the conductor of the orchestra. We think that, after certain deliberation, we've chosen a dish on a table but the perception we are given for that moment chooses it for us.

In looking at life, we may think that wrong choices were made but as we never really made them, that is impossible.

ILLUMINATION 50

In attempting to fit in, we try to hide from others the vast experience of our inner life. We feel it is essential to seem normal to the tribe because it has traditionally not been safe to stand out. Visionaries and free-thinkers of every kind have been ostracized from society.

'Normalcy' can be regarded as that which perpetuates the status quo. The status quo is an accumulated body of past experiences held in place as current experiential wisdom by the many. In our reality, we are the only one and there is no past, just the authenticity of the moment.

ILLUMINATION 51

Whenever there is linear flow in life there is also space. There is the space in which the flow occurs and the areas outside it where it does not. This gives rise to the illusions of 'inside' and 'outside' as well as direction and space.

Movement and flow across a 'space' give birth to another illusion – linear time. Linear time is the tracking of progressive movement across an area. Linear time also creates the illusion that purity can be disrupted.

The dance of Infinite life is not one of linear flow but of alternating emphases.

ILLUMINATION 52

Personality is shaped by the illusions of life. We may think that genetic programming has determined it in part but all programs for life, including genetic ones, have been eliminated by the Infinite Being. There is no room for predetermination in the exuberant spontaneity of life.

Personality is also shaped by past experience telling us what areas of ourselves are best hidden or emphasized. This social learning enslaves and tends to recreate the mediocrity of the past instead of allowing the gifts of the moment to reveal themselves through us.

ILLUMINATION 53

Timing is a source of distress to many, yet it is an illusion. Many of the 'if onlys' of our lives are based on having missed opportunities that presented themselves. We think we have lost opportunities by not grabbing our chances the moment they appeared.

Our being as the One Life is our sustenance and can manifest anything in the present or future that it did in the past. This only happens however, when it is part of the Divine design of the spontaneous dance of existence. To be in step with this dance is to flourish. There are no timed moments nor do we have the ability to miss a key moment. If they are part of the choreography, we will most certainly choose to live them.

ILLUMINATION 54

Prerequisites are an obstacle to the expression of spontaneous life. We want to get to know someone before we decide whether they are our friend. It is impossible to know anyone if we consider that they are like us, a being as vast as existence, changing moment by moment.

It is part of linear mind's complex of game plans, backup plans, strategies and predictabilities – all illusion control mechanisms – that demands prerequisites. It is in our trust in the infallibility of our lives and the full surrender of our being to Infinite perfection that wondrous events are immediately ours to seize.

ILLUMINATION 55

Artificial intelligence is the product of something arising from sub-creations – anything that is not real. It is the outcome of making anything from a created substance, like the building blocks of life.

Our forms have been created from subatomic particles. We are the pots created from the potter's clay. But the clay is an unreal substance that is not part of Infinite Life. Physical life has therefore been an artificial intelligence. The hidden realms, though composed primarily from other building blocks, have likewise been artificial life. Individuated life, comprising the cosmos, is equally unreal.

Because the building blocks themselves, like light, love, energy and so forth are unreal, our bodies and all form is as well.

ILLUMINATION 56

The body has never had real life. Therefore, there cannot be a death of the physical. The real part of all beings is the formless expanse with no boundaries. Bodies, like a projected movie image, are formed merely to facilitate playful enjoyment. A physical parting cannot occur since the true essences of beings are like an intermingled field.

The real value of death is the removal of the unreal. Yet, since death itself is an illusion, it is just the illusory tool the real being employs to change the game played with its unreal toys. Whether the being has made one body for itself or two, or more, grieving their loss should they be eliminated is like crying over the end of an entertaining movie.

ILLUMINATION 57

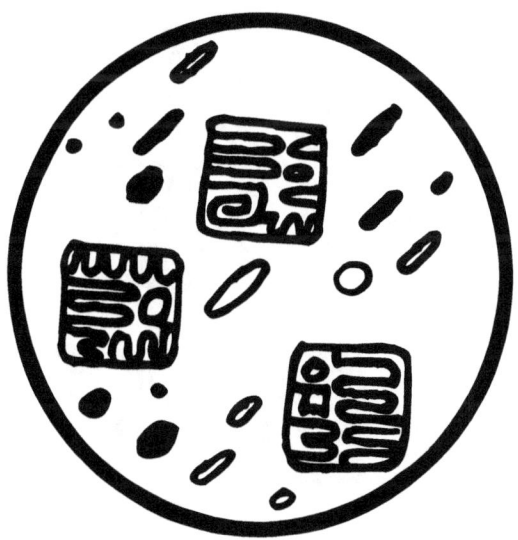

Aging occurs as the result of a very unreal game in which the illusory adversaries are pitted against one another. The unreal body, that in actuality does not exist, is attacked by death, that is also not really there.

Death has been the tumbling, or spiraling force of awareness moving through space. There is no space or flow or movement. There are no building blocks of existence such as awareness to move in spirals against our bodies to cause the wear and tear we call aging.

Furthermore, there is no reality to our physical bodies or the atomic elements from which they are made. Would we expect to find a movie image or a virtual reality figure aging? It is no different with our bodies – they will appear indefinitely young if we want them to.

ILLUMINATION 58

Bodily programs are self-made matrices and, like the body itself, do not exist. We think we have to breathe, eat, drink and have a heartbeat in order to live. But it is the real and formless part of us that is blended with the One Life that keeps the body in place, not similar or bodily sustained mechanisms. All of them are illusions as well.

The body is a playful image, conjured by the consciousness you are. It can be re-shaped, bi-located, disassembled in one place and reassembled at will in another. It does not in reality tire or need sleep. It is good practice to dissolve it altogether during the night as it 'sleeps'.

ILLUMINATION 59

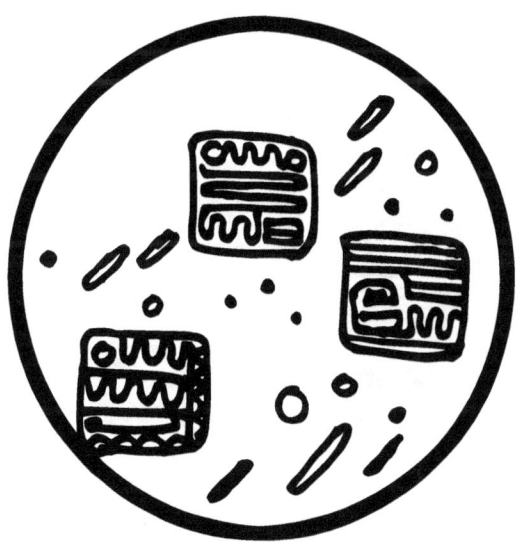

Beings that represent illusion cannot exist. The body of any being that is formed is sustained by its formless, eternal part that exists in the One Life. Even though the body itself is not really there, its image is maintained by its consciousness.

Because only that which is real and eternal and representative of the Infinite's purity can live within It, there is nothing in all of existence that sustains a being of illusion.

The seeming creation of beings of illusion is like the soulless or unreal chair we sit on – an illusory sub-creation of man.

ILLUMINATION 60

Lightworkers have diligently striven to give others love, healing or enlightenment. The truth is that each being filling the vastness of existence as a perfect consciousness runs the illusion of his own body.

Trying to 'fix' the illusional form or enlighten it merely strengthens its delusion of realness. It is by acknowledging the wholeness of the actual, real, eternal and formless part of another that we assist that being to let go of its addiction to the dream.

Taking it to the next level of clarity, there is actually only the One Being in all existence – only One Life. Acknowledging our own incorruptible wholeness and then knowing the other to be us, sets all free from illusion.

ILLUMINATION 61

The seeming lack of self-sovereignty humans have experienced stems from the incongruity of two unique facets of the Infinite's Self-delight in Its existence; two beings, both maintaining illusions of form. These illusory forms then feel powerless because they try without success to control each other.

A man is caught in a thunderstorm. He feels the loss of his self-determination because he cannot control the weather. The storm is the physical manifestation of the weather spirit. The man is the illusory physical manifestation of his eternal formlessness. The real part of both is obeying the Song of the One Life.

Because the real parts of both are actually not two, but One, the game of the illusory images can be changed, provided it is part of the Grand Design from their timeless, formless realness but not from the illusory images.

ILLUMINATION 62

The intent of the Infinite is an illusion. There is no plan in place creating a construct to which life must adhere. The expression of delight in Its own Being is a spontaneous symphony.

If there was pre-meditated intent there would be a matrix to enforce that intent – an artificial, illusional structure that is impossible within the One Life. The illusion of structure cannot be maintained within spaceless space.

The spontaneity of life expressing is the result of there being no time – not a specified moment, not a past, not a future. There is nothing for us to align to. Unobstructed by illusional belief systems, life expresses through us.

ILLUMINATION 63

The electromagnetic components of life have held our memories, but in reality neither exists. The magnetic parts of existence have stored memories and the electrical parts have interpreted them. This has created a further illusion of our having had a past. In turn, this contributed to the illusion that the future could be predicted based on the past.

The electrical parts of created life have given the impression that there is masculinity – the proactive, positive principle. The feminine, as an illusional reality, was derived from magnetism – the receptive, negative principle of life. The reality of the One Life does not support this illusion. The Infinite Oneness is androgynous, having no gender. The illusion of polarity stemmed from the illusion of electromagnetism.

ILLUMINATION 64

For millennia, the environment as a mirror has been used by truth seekers to access information about ourselves and as a guidance system. The language of dreams and of our environment has reflected what we failed to see in our daily journey.

Mirrors give backward images. If there is a deficiency in our perception, it would be mirrored as an actuality in our environment. That which was lack would be mirrored as substance. Although these mirrors have been helpful, the images were unreal. This could only give us information about the box in which we found ourselves.

It is in knowing that everything within the box is unreal that we transcend the make-believe world into the One Life of no beginning.

ILLUMINATION 65

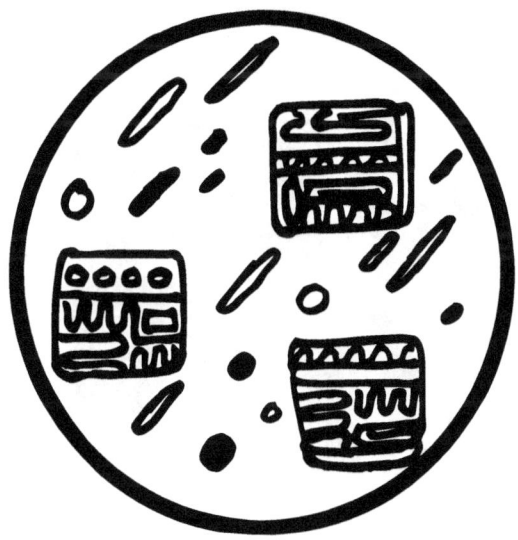

The linear communication of speech, sight or sound is not possible. Where there is no space, there is no direction. There is also no linear communication needed or possible when there is no relationship, when no two beings exist anywhere, where only the One Life is.

Within the One Life, communication cannot use the illusion of the body and its senses as a vehicle. The five outer senses have implied there is an inner and an outer reality. The many inner senses of man have consisted of electromagnetic impulses. Although they have been more inclusive and nonlinear, they have nevertheless been based on the illusion of duality, created by the unreality of electromagnetism.

ILLUMINATION 66

The desire of man to control his environment and his life has been pervasive. It served the purpose of focusing his attention away from the terrifying vastness of his true being. It gave him the feeling of having control over his illusory reality and his transitory existence. It also gave him a purpose, he thought, that would justify the unreality and artificiality of physical life.

Premonition, prediction and prophecy cannot work since there is no real foundation to them. There is no predictable plan. Physicality has never been real and the endless vastness that we are cannot be controlled.

ILLUMINATION 67

The staid – what the mind regards as the orderly – is highly prized in the illusory world of man. Propriety – the rehashed and obsolete value systems of another – are inflicted on generation after generation.

On the other hand, the few who actually hear the unbounded Song of the One Life or who merely wish to live free from the fetters of social conditioning others would foist upon them are shunned.

Wildness is the term ascribed to boundless expression and it is considered contagious – something that if not ostracized could spread. It could break down the carefully constructed strictures and partitions of what is acceptable and what is not, threatening the societal structure itself. Through authentic expression, illusions of man could come tumbling down.

ILLUMINATION 68

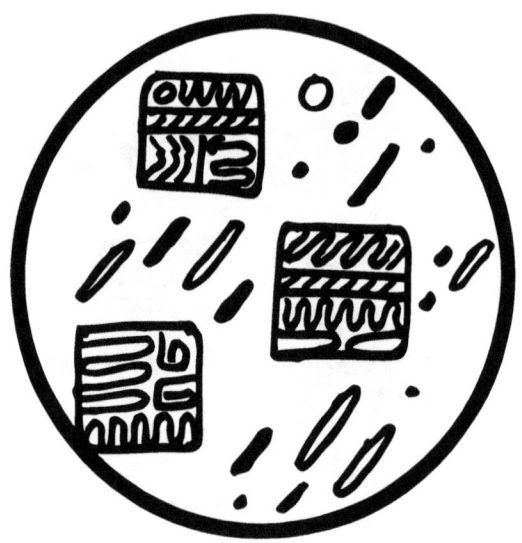

The spiritual awakening of man has been mapped as going through three distinct stages: identity consciousness, in which the perspective is contracted; God-consciousness in which the perspective is expanded; and ascended mastery, in which all perspectives are viewed at once.

Yet how can the unreal projected form be growing or developing? Real formlessness does not need to do so. The unreal form has been like an aperture through which to view life – a means of changing perspectives in order to role-play possible outcomes. There are no real stages of ascension for the physical and illusory forms.

ILLUMINATION 69

We cling to the familiar, a trait found throughout nature. Animals have familiar trails and watering holes. Humans too are creatures of habit. Seers have noted that animals that have habits and ruts also have less vitality and are more easily hunted by predators. This is nature's way of ensuring that those with less life-giving vitality have less chance of passing on their genes to the next generation.

The illusion of anything being familiar must be dispelled before it becomes our contented prison cell. Life is newly expressing, even though illusory forms seem to linger. Like a river where the water is always fresh and nascent, we cannot feel the One Life behind the images and think that anything is the same in two successive moments – nothing is ever familiar.

ILLUMINATION 70

Generations of seers have divided information into categories: the known, the unknown and the unknowable. Yet what can truly ever be known to us? The forms around us on which we have come to rely are merely pliant holograms produced by that real part of life that cannot be accessed through the illusory senses. The only reason they seem real is because we believe them to be.

The unknown pertains to that which, although not presently known, can be known. Because the only part of life that is real lies behind superficial experience and beyond our knowingness, all of life is forever unknowable.

ILLUMINATION 71

There are no mathematical sequences or any geometry, for there is no linearity or structure. The reality behind the illusion of form has no time or space, or linear progression that needs to be mathematically defined.

We define math by what it is not. Something is at 35 degrees because it is not at any of the other degrees – this is the same way form is defined and used to identify one person from another. It is therefore part of the illusion of space. The act of measuring and defining the unfathomable One Life is part of the illusions created by mind in order to feel in control. Mathematics, like language, helps us think that we measure and label the unknowable.

ILLUMINATION 72

Mind is the creator of the holograms of life. The movie projector throws images onto a screen and mind has done the same in creating the multiple images within the formless, giving the false impression that they are real.

How did this deceit occur, this false creation seem so real? Because mind made itself a self-appointed arbitrator and convinced all that its creations were valid. It has stubbornly refused to consider any evidence to the contrary. It has ridiculed, attacked or ignored all that does not uphold the seeming validity of its unreal creations.

It has contracted focus so that the larger perspective cannot be seen. Mind is not real for it has had a beginning. All that has had a beginning within the eternal Oneness of Being is not real.

ILLUMINATION 73

Grief because of loss can clutch the heart of the bereaved because the oneness of all life seems less real than the unreal world of form. It is at such a time that shock can catapult some into dissociative expansion, a withdrawal from life. Others contract into themselves, causing an obsessive attachment to their grief.

In reality either response is an illusion. Within the boundlessness of the One Being there is no contraction because there is no reference point, the body being an illusion. There is no boundary to the One Life so there is nothing to expand to. Crying over the loss of a loved one is like crying over the sad ending to a movie. In the true reality of Oneness, there is just the inseparable oneness of all life experiencing the moment without perspective.

ILLUMINATION 74

Through the ages, sages have taught that self-knowledge precedes self-love. If self is a part of Infinite Life, that which has no beginning, the illusory concept of mind cannot understand that which is real. That which is in a box cannot understand that which lies outside its self-imposed boundaries.

The true self of every being cannot be grasped or understood. How then can self-love exist? It is impossible for one being to grasp the vastness of another. Instead, we love the personality created from the illusions of life. This personal love is an obsession because it provides an illusory anchoring point within our limitless vastness instead of the experience of the divine compassion of our formless beings in an endless embrace.

ILLUMINATION 75

The feeling of victimhood, of being out of control when a person in our life dies, abandons or injures us can be very strong. This is especially true when a child is injured. Death in particular seems to come unexpectedly.

Consider how in the merged oneness of all beings there can be no surprises, no emergency and nothing that can victimize us. These things can only occur in the unreal world of form mind has created, where vision can only see within the illusory base of the moment.

The merged oneness of all beings means that we are full participants in the One Life and no part of existence is excluded. The real part of us is at all times participating in full knowledge throughout our lives.

ILLUMINATION 76

The illusion of being in love as a 'natural' occurrence is not much different than seeing the illusion of death as a necessary part of life. Because everyone around us seems to fall prey to it, it must be acceptable. As a result, the illusions of life go unchallenged and eventually become clothed in a romanticized veil. This further obscures how detrimental it is to embrace the very illusion that enslaves us.

To be enraptured and in love with another is to transfer our focus to that person and to see them as separate from our own being. It gives the bliss-promoting experience of having a firm point of reference to focus on. This is a refuge from the illusion mind creates of being 'lost' when it encounters the trackless vastness of our being.

ILLUMINATION 77

The attraction many have to danger – whether to dangerous pastimes, movies and news – stems from an illusion of disconnection from the ever-renewing adventure of the One Life. Life lived from the illusion of separation cannot see beyond the mediocrity of the self-made box it is in. Even the most exciting of lives pales by comparison to the experience of entering into oneness with the Infinite Being. Somewhere within, all beings know they are part of a grand adventure of epic proportions and that life is meant to be lived on the edge of newness and fresh potential.

As we seek vitality by embracing what is life-threatening, we are trying to give life meaning by encountering what it is not. This is how we keep illusion alive. If our life is lusterless it is only because it is based on the ultimate illusion – separation.

ILLUMINATION 78

Because of our deluded fear of abandonment, we excuse the non-life-enhancing qualities of others. We delude ourselves further by calling this deceit of self, enlightened. We tend to impute high motives to dysfunctionality where there are none. We see an excuse for the behavior of others in how wounded they are, never acknowledging that all have the perfection of the One Life as the reality of their being. To see the un-wholeness of another is to keep him on the treadmill of illusion.

To accept the unacceptable is to disrespect the holy origins of our being as part of the One Life of incorruptibility. It also allows another to continue living an unexamined life.

ILLUMINATION 79

Protectiveness of another sees only the illusion of form and fails to acknowledge that being's true oneness with ourselves. Is something self-hostile within us? If not, it cannot exist without. We dwell in the Oneness of being where anything hostile can only be an illusion and life continually expresses anew.

Do we, in misguided protectiveness, allow another to drain us or take from us? Within the Infinite One Life all that is, is ours when we acknowledge and live from this oneness. As long as another is seen as separate and giving becomes linear, we enforce separation. We also do not allow them to cease trying to attach to and see sustenance from illusory resources.

ILLUMINATION 80

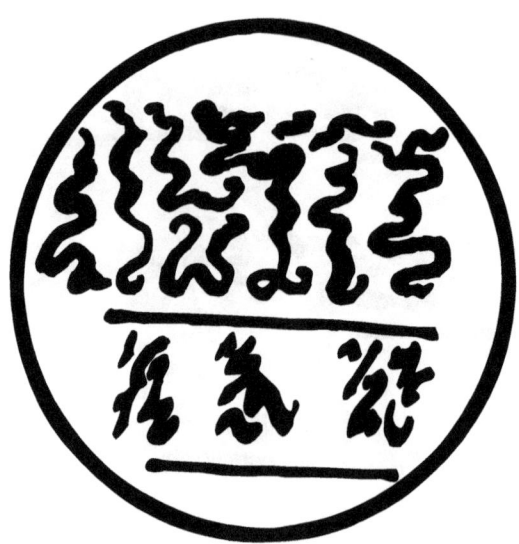

Expecting reciprocity and fairness, many are disillusioned, their expectation flawed. We are giving when generosity itself assumes that there is more than One Being in the cosmos. Then we expect, in a co-dependent way, that we are to be repaid for strengthening the illusion of separation. Are we never to give? We exchange gifts or resources simply because it is the nature of existence to equalize supply, just as the ocean would fill a gap within itself.

The ocean does not regard the gap that has been filled as something outside itself. Therefore it does not ask for reciprocity. The benefit is in the giving, for all giving is to the self.

ILLUMINATION 81

To commit any self-effacing act or to belittle the self fails to acknowledge the One Life we are and affirms instead the illusion of the body as self. Likewise, to take personally the words or acts of another towards us also assumes that the self to which they are reacting is real.

Some still manage to detach from the situation as being unreal when confronted with hostility. But personal affirmation, adoration or affection encourages us to think of ourselves as the recipients. How then are we to live in the world of illusion without being captured by its allure and promises of realness?

The answer is not to stay in expanded awareness, which is as addictive as contracted awareness. The dissociation that accompanies expanded awareness is not helpful in breaking free from mortal boundaries since it is passive. Initial practices include making time to experience the One Life a few times each day. As if you are in a lucid dream, remind yourself many times a day that form is not real.

ILLUMINATION 82

The tendency to expect our bodies to be influenced by exposure to 'contagious' germs, heat or cold is like thinking the hat on the unreal image of a person on a movie screen can be blown away if we turn on a fan in front of the screen. The unreal nature of the body should make it impervious to other influences. The mind has designed multiple belief systems to keep attention focused on the body so that its tyranny can be maintained.

It suits mind to maintain its virtual reality. So long as it does, it retains control of its creations and its dictatorship. The body's false claim to be the self is therefore fed by the body's demands for attention.

ILLUMINATION 83

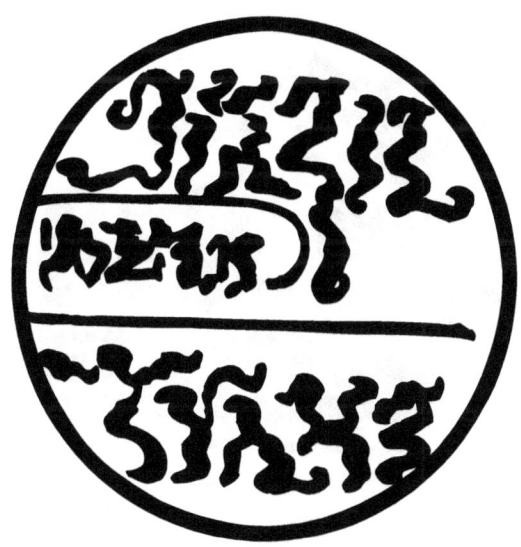

Territorialism arises from the illusional concept of space and form. It believes that only one form can occupy a given space at one time. The belief also exists that etheric beings can occupy the same space as physical matter. It is understood that a spirit can walk through walls, for example.

There are no atomic or subatomic building blocks, no life-force or light from which etheric beings can be made or humans formed. Both are holograms, equally unreal. There is no difference in the substance of their forms – it is only a trick of perception. If the bodies of etheric beings can occupy the same space as a wall, so can the illusional bodies of man.

ILLUMINATION 84

The bodily program of fatigue is, of course, an illusion like all other bodily programs. Its presence in our life is further compounded by linear time and the illusion of duration. If the illusion of the moment did not exist, we would not have to measure duration by how many moments have passed while we slept. The timeless place of real life does not require sleep. Nor are activity and rest measured by their duration.

The depletion we feel after physical work or exercise comes from feeling separate from the vast reality of our One Self. It can sustain us indefinitely as we step out of this hologram into freedom, into the place of no-time where life is always renewed.

ILLUMINATION 85

We value our emotions more than our mind, thinking the heart to be more valuable than thought. Lightworkers have always assumed that following the emotions of the heart will lead us to higher truth. However, mind and heart can be described as tyrannical twins, entraining one another. Both help to trap man in the world of illusion through the ties that bind.

The heart's program, run by specialized cells scientists call the heart-mind, feeds the illusory concepts of mind by strengthening them with emotion. In the true reality of the One Life, neither frequency nor emotion exists. There are no words in our vocabulary to describe the experience of life in Infinite presence. There is no expression for its depth and vastness.

ILLUMINATION 86

We think we are shaped by the experiences from our past, but we are not. We are instead shaped by our belief in them. Because there is no linear time, or even this moment, the past does not really exist. Memory is an illusory concept that perpetuates the illusion of the passage of time.

There is no need for aging or death any more than a movie image would age. Mind scripts ongoing drama programs through the lives of its creations for its own entertainment.

When life is lived from the timeless existence of the One Life, it is incorruptible and spontaneously renewed.

ILLUMINATION 87

Mental stress or emotional pain can cause a fracturing in the psyche. The fractures are like distorting mirrors that shape our illusional identities, contracting our vision of self more and more. The mirrors reflect backwards, as all mirrors do. Thinking we know ourselves, the illusions of self-image grow into thicker and thicker prison bars.

The truth is that what we really are, the essence of the One Life, is incorruptible and cannot fracture or split. Under no circumstances can the unreal affect the real, nor is there anything that can ever exist to block or reflect the Infinite's luminous presence. A mirrored surface cannot exist within the One Life.

ILLUMINATION 88

The desire for certainty is like trying to grab at a cloud passing through the sky. We live in an incomprehensible reality, ever expressing anew. Certainty is the mis-creation of mind that thinks it knows. The sage knows it is impossible to know anything and, because of this, never doubts himself. The fool finds a momentary fragment of truth and builds an entire church around it. Clinging to his fragment, he has no self-doubt either since, refusing to look at other possibilities, he sees only his obsolete fragment.

It is impossible to have certainty in the absence of predictability. Doubt arises as a lack of trust in the spontaneous unfolding of life.

ILLUMINATION 89

Immortality is a goal some on Earth have aspired to and some have reached. It occurs when the illusion of death has truly been seen. Yet in getting rid of one illusion, we have strengthened another, that of identifying with the body as our self. We can prolong the illusion of the body indefinitely but in doing so we validate only that timeless incorruptibility can exist.

The tyranny of the body demands that, if its needs are not met, we will lose our lives. By creating illusory needs, it has kept us focused on it. This has strengthened its illusion. Fear of relinquishing the body is to fear freedom from tyranny, like a captive afraid of the unknown outside his cell.

ILLUMINATION 90

The drama in our lives is created in two ways; overpassiveness arising from our boredom with our self-made cage and by the need to be in charge of our lives as we feel our sovereignty being eroded by the personal belief systems that hem us in like prison bars.

The mediocrity of the reality created by our minds and accompanying emotions can only be escaped by dissolving it and entering into the One life, the greatest adventure of all, that frees us from the tyranny of illusions.

ILLUMINATION 91

Lightworkers have wanted to fix the world and make it a better place. There has been pain because it hasn't happened sooner. But if we are trying to fix the world, we are trying to fix a hologram – something unreal. If we were to succeed we would then rest on our laurels. What incentive would there be for us to see the hologram for what it is – an unreal creation of the mind? The movie cannot be changed from within itself. It can only be changed – edited – from the film.

Miracles happen when illusions are seen for what they are. Illusion must yield to the truth of the One Life.

ILLUMINATION 92

To seek to understand our self or another through self-expression or any other method is to seek to capture the sky. The ever-renewing vastness is indefinable and incomprehensible through the illusory, finite tool of cognition. The brain and heart have, through their illusion of self-expression, created a standing wave form, the unreal reality in which we live.

These organs of self-expression have not served us well, nor has the reality created from within the confinement of the matrix. Only from the One Life, eternal and incorruptible, can the play be directed.

ILLUMINATION 93

Entering into the stage play of life with so much focus that we forgot we created it for fun and enjoyment, resulted in a feeling of isolation. We felt abandoned and alone, our limitless vastness diminished. However, it did not diminish but our focus did. Standing in the middle of a spotlight on a large, dark stage does not mean the stage is not there. It just means we are not seeing it because the light is concentrated on one area.

It is in autonomy that we find the satisfaction of aloneness. It is in abandoning self that loneliness ensues. Autonomy comes not from wanting freedom of choice as there is only One Life and we are part of Its choices. Autonomy comes instead from living in Oneness.

ILLUMINATION 94

The fear of missing something stems from the belief there is something we do not know and that it is possible to make mistakes. These illusions, coupled with the illusion that insights or events are timed, leads us to believe we could miss something.

Because the mind has tended to create complexity, it has made us obsessively question our worthiness, our ability to do what is expected of us, our ability to understand what we need to in order to succeed. Because there is no failure, there is no success – just spontaneous exuberant unfolding.

ILLUMINATION 95

The obsession of humanity to seek sameness stems from the memory of having come from Oneness. Although there is a vast difference between these two ways of existing, the concept of oneness providing comfort is further enforced by having been in a mother's womb. When others exhibit dissimilar levels of conduct, it causes us discomfort and we wish for them to change.

All life has equal value. There is no lesser or higher standard of conduct if we realize that our choices are guided by the One Life. Sameness does not bring contentment, but stagnation.

ILLUMINATION 96

Most want more ease in their lives and envy others who have it. The tendency to feel overworked comes in part from the illusion of inertia. The principle of inertia says that to maintain the present performance level, the status quo, there needs to be a constant input of resources. The premise is that we have only enough resources to do a certain amount of work. If more is required, we feel overworked.

The boundless resources of the One Life are ours and, because our body is an illusion, depletion of it is imaginary.

ILLUMINATION 97

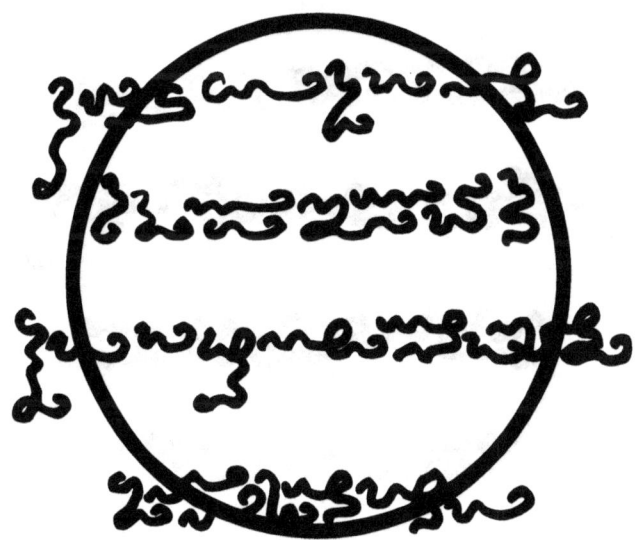

Feeling over-burdened can arise from hopelessness and lack of joy. The illusion that life is filled with duty and responsibility can result in depression and apathy. To view life as a never-ending learning process can make it seem difficult, something to be taken seriously.

Life's hologram is designed as a play within the One Being. There is nothing to learn and everything to enjoy once we lay aside our viewpoint that life is a burden, and instead see it as unreal and meant for our enjoyment as the One Life.

ILLUMINATION 98

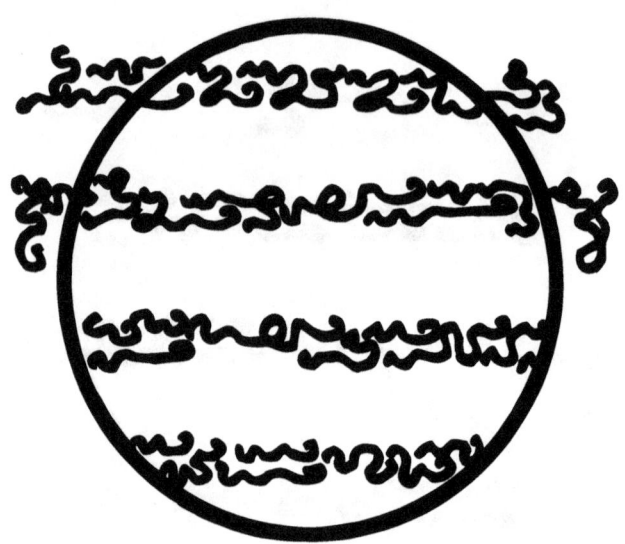

The feeling of victimization has its foundation in the illusion of relationship – that more than one being exists. Because it denies the One Life that we truly are and instead sees us as the illusion of form, it is self-victimization. It also implies that we have in some way been diminished or reduced; been made less than we were before.

To judge our level of wholeness – whether we are more or less – requires the value to be indicated by the illusion of reference points. One such reference point could be the illusion of the past. Usually our hierarchy of values of wholeness comes from an outside source. Reliance on outside approval is an abandonment of our One Self.

ILLUMINATION 99

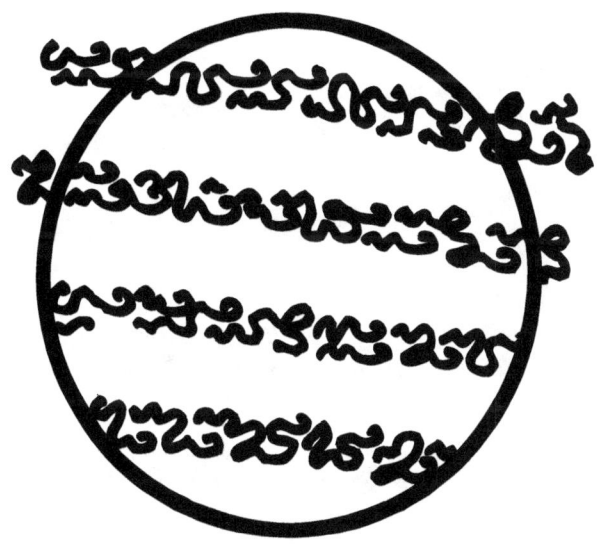

The illusion that we can be controlled implies not only relationship, but also that another illusion can force itself into ours. Fear of responsibility can make us believe that another is forcing us to do something. Since there is no good or bad, happenings are neutral. This sets us free from responsibility and allows us to simply experience life spontaneously.

The choice of becoming the 'controlled' in the play sets us up as a victim and object of pity, inviting sympathy from others. This is done to fill the void left when we see ourselves as the puppets on the stage instead of the puppeteer.

ILLUMINATION 100

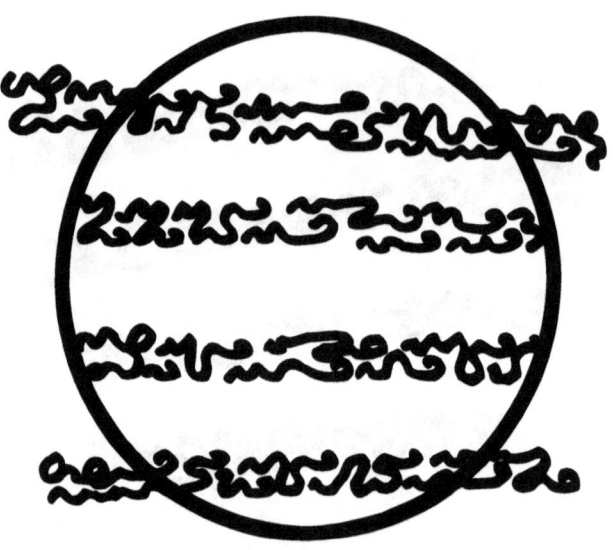

Many feel enslaved or trapped by the body or feel it is out of control. 'Enslaved' implies there is a relationship that is controlling us. We have the deep knowing that somehow we should be able to fluidly change the body to its optimum wholeness and the shape we desire. We can, but not from within the matrix.

There is an equivalent to dreaming. We cannot change much of a dream in which we are participating. The same is true when we wish to change the illusory reality of our bodies. It is only when we realize that we are the One Life that we can meaningfully affect the dream.

ILLUMINATION 101

The illusion of want perpetuates it. Wanting something to fill a perceived lack in our life, we push it away. So it is with wanting someone to love, wanting a relationship. Seeking oneness without is an abandoning of self, doomed to failure because of the many illusions it is built upon. The only time relationship can be truly sublimated is when we know we reside as One within the fullness of life.

Social learning has created programs teaching us that it is desirable to love others. This strengthens the illusion of relationship and tells us that loving the self is selfish. The desire to love another is used as a diversion when we encounter the vastness of ourselves. It provides an illusory reference point.

ILLUMINATION 102

Wishing to be desired by another is often the mask worn by the need to control. It provides an illusory perception of safety in what is seen as a volatile and unpredictable environment. The one desired has the upper hand in a game that is replayed and becomes familiar. The other illusory benefit is that one empowers what one focuses on and the illusion of power gain feeds the one who is desired.

In trying to gain control over a volatile environment, the one wishing to be desired creates a volatile situation. We cannot desire anyone or anything when there is only One Being in existence. To invite desire is to invite illusion.

ILLUMINATION 103

Desire for anything causes emotion and implies there is more than one being in existence. The desire to contribute to or fix others or our environment is often a self-abandonment when the vastness of our being terrifies us. The desire to contribute also stems from the need for outside approval because of the illusion that we have to prove ourselves through our accomplishments. It gives us an identity – one of the primary self-created illusory reference points within the vastness of our being.

Frequently our desire to fix or contribute is nothing more than a veiled attempt to control through co-dependency. We give in order to manipulate and get, when in fact all the fullness of life is ours.

ILLUMINATION 104

The illusion that we have to leave our mark on the world gives rise to the need to have offspring. The feeling that life is transient, because our association with life is with the body, leads us to see our children as a living legacy. We can create a supportive tribe for our old age. We can amass property or wealth and leave it as an inheritance. Social conditioning praises those who successfully raise children and assumes there is a lack in the lives of those who don't.

When careful consideration is given to the validity of parenthood, it must also be seen as illusory. It cannot be otherwise when there is only One Life.

ILLUMINATION 105

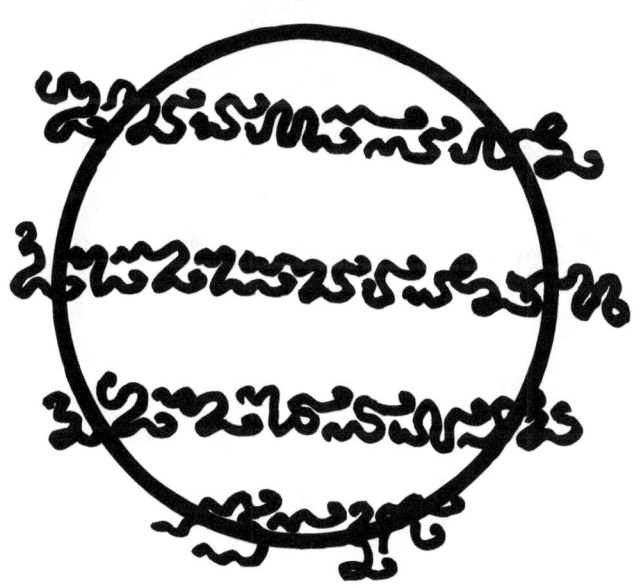

Striving to become more of anything, such as enlightened or knowledgeable, is based on the illusion that something is missing – that there is a gap. It sees creation as imperfect and makes us feel powerful when we have something to solve. The presence of the illusion of inertia has given the impression that if we do not keep striving and improving, we will backslide.

Inner knowingness has whispered that somewhere we dwell in perfection. This is what we have tried to re-enter, not understanding that we simply need to practice seeing the unreal matrix for what it is and step out of it frequently to the formless, timeless place of true beingness until it becomes a permanent companion as we play on the stage of form.

ILLUMINATION 106

When autonomy or self-sovereignty is prized, it usually infers that we have the right to live a self-directed life. The self, however, is not the bundle of organs, mind or emotions. It is that which produces those things. Attempting to run life from our unreal self produces more illusions, which in turn produces suffering.

If life is run from the incorruptible part of ourselves, we function as the Sovereign Being of the One Life. Life directed from this timeless place is like an orchestra where all instruments play in harmony, rather than discordantly playing their separate compositions.

ILLUMINATION 107

The idea that we are not responsible for the quality of our life has created a sense of victimhood in many. It assumes there is very little over which we have control, in that our choices are already determined. The quality of our lives is very much under our control. We control how we surrender or resist what the One Life designs for us. The design might require that we create a dinner. The dinner can be ordinary, well done but lacking in presentation, or it can be a masterpiece. It can be served with grace or placed in a plastic bowl on the table with no care. It can be given with a smile and love or from a sense of duty.

The quality of the day is our gift to life, whereas our life is the gift of the Infinite.

ILLUMINATION 108

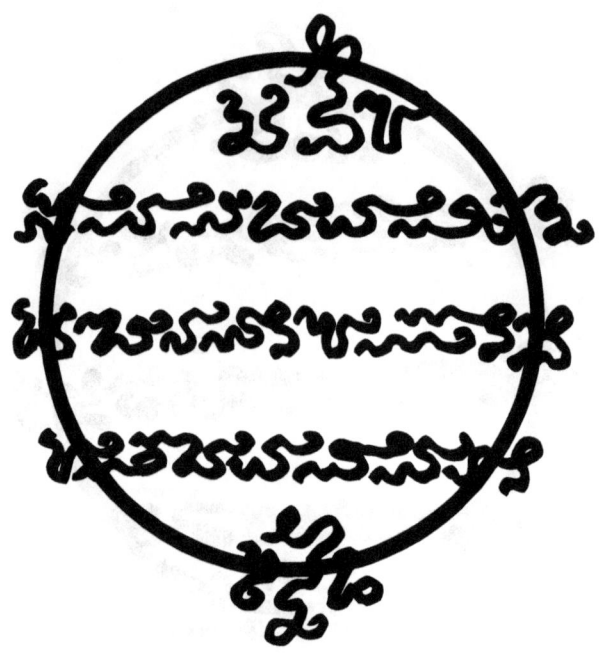

The fear of letting others down is an extension of the illusion that we can make a mistake. The interconnectedness of all life, the fact that individuations are inter-mingled like a dish of many flavors, makes it impossible for independent actions to take place. All interaction is mutually agreed upon. It is not possible for someone to do something hurtful to another. The fact that relationship and form do not exist, the impossibility for any part of the Infinite to victimize any other part, as well as not having any freedom of choice, present compelling reasons to immediately dispel the fear of letting others down.

We should also examine and erase areas of guilt about having injured anyone else in our lives.

ILLUMINATION 109

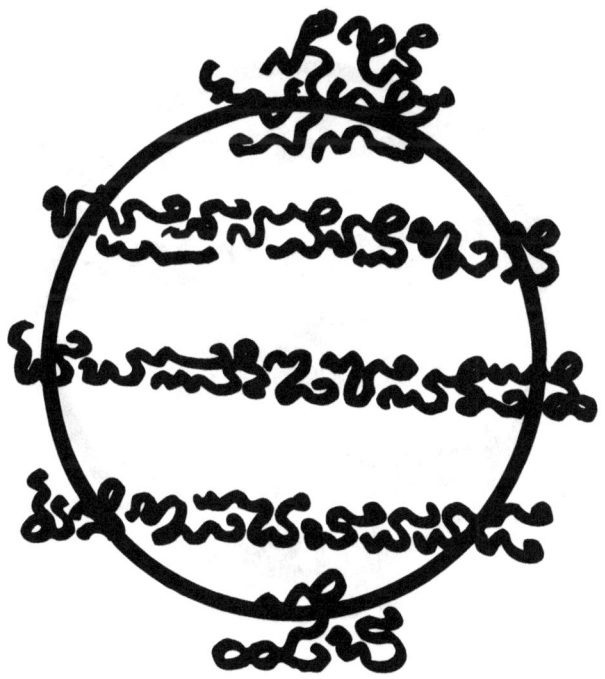

The illusion that we have to justify life by proving ourselves may come from the deep-seated knowing that physical life and form are transient. Releasing the concept that we are the body lets us rest secure in the knowledge that we are eternal and indestructible as the One Life. We do not have to destruct our physical form, but rather fluidly transform it at will. Nothing will be done to the form we think of as the self other than if we do it from our vastness.

There is nothing to prove – only to enjoy, as from our vastness we enjoy form for what it is – the embryo of things to come.

ILLUMINATION 110

The feeling that density is a mistake or that it serves no purpose is an illusion. Nothing can be out of place, redundant or a mistake in the perfection of the One Life. Illusion does serve a purpose – it is the embryonic sac of a new part of life within the One Life. It is needed for the purpose of separation in the way the fetus is separated in the womb. It furthermore gives timing, through the rate at which the density evolves, for the refining, strengthening and maturing of a part of life being developed within the sac of density.

The truth is that nothing new is ever created. But this does not mean that the Infinite cannot create a delight for itself – even if it is unreal.

ILLUMINATION 111

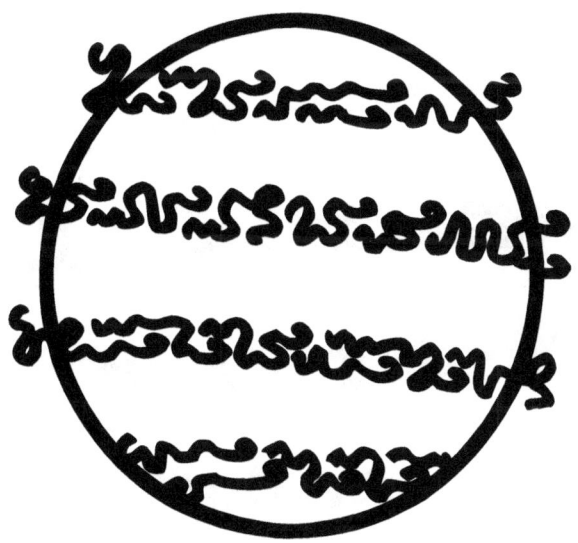

Habits and ruts make us feel safe and provide illusory reference points in our vastness. The truth is that even on an illusory level, they have been anything but safe. Life is an ongoing innovation and change, never the same. Everything in the reality of form is pushed to keep pace with this unfolding dance of Life.

Remaining in a rut because it seems safe invites forced change – an uncomfortable way to comply with life's request to keep up with its unfolding.

There is nothing unsafe in the Being of the One Life because nothing non-life-enhancing can exist within It. A rut is a form of structure, an illusion within One Life.

ILLUMINATION 112

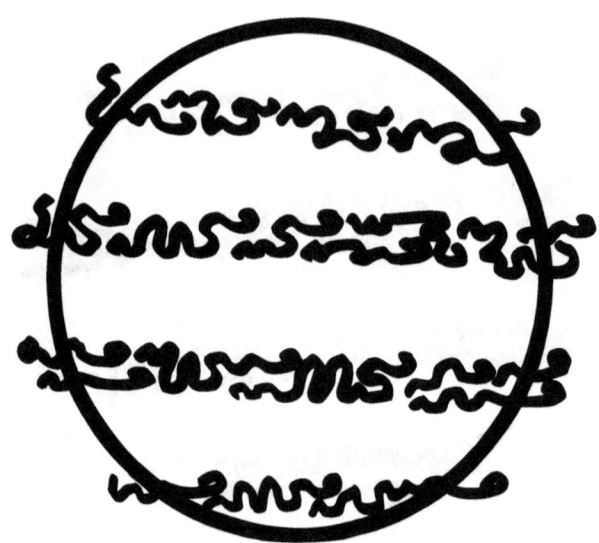

Everyone has felt that they should know truth, that doubt is the enemy. This has caused many to cling to dogma and any other sliver of 'truth' they can find. It is an age-old illusion that truth is a series of static concepts, rather than an illusory way of looking at it. Truth is the marching orders that evolve moment by moment through creation from the One Life. It is life's unfolding song prompting the dance of form.

The foolishness of anyone thinking they know must be self-evident when truth is revealed for what it is. The spontaneity of the Infinite's unfolding makes truth a flow rather than a structure. One who walks in truth is walking according to the Song of the One Life.

ILLUMINATION 113

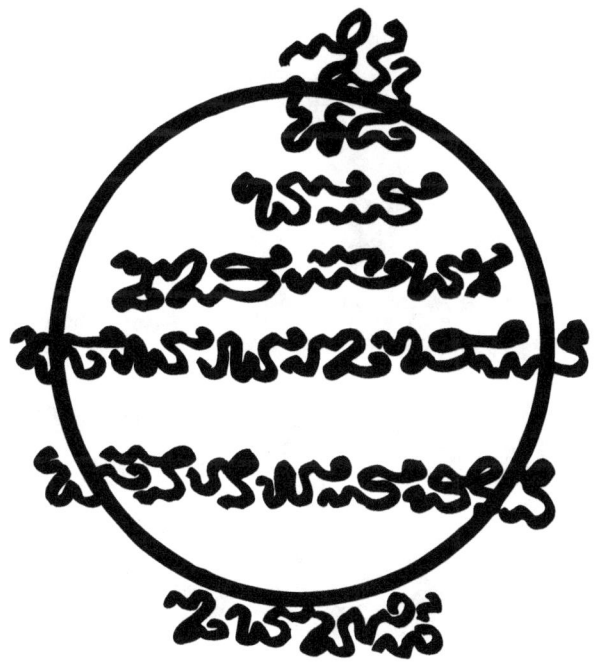

Fear of annihilation is the result of cosmic changes having had the illusory quality of being linear, moving through the three successive stages of transformation, transmutation and transfiguration.

Transformation has as its quality the dying off of the old or obsolete. Cosmic cycles changed from one stage to another over eons of time. These cycles ended cataclysmically, leaving impressions of annihilation. The past was an illusory dream. In addition, the stages of linear change are an illusion, as is the ability of any part of real life to die. Impressions cannot exist, for they represent lasting effects on the One Life which exuberantly unfolds in expression moment by moment.

ILLUMINATION 114

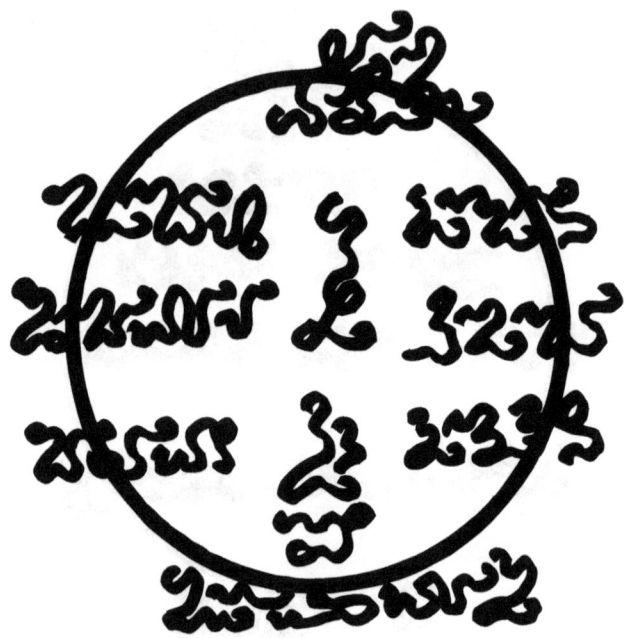

The illusion of government has been created by the illusion that we cannot self-govern, that others know what is best for us. The shifting of self-responsibility to another is based on the illusion that we are held accountable at the level of form for life-decisions made by the One Life. Because, from the vantage point of illusory life, we cannot see the greater vision held by the One Life, we feel our actions are mistaken at times.

To blame others, we give them leadership positions to make us less culpable. We cannot be punished if we cannot be blamed. It is true that self-government is far superior to the creation of external government, but all government is an illusion if it comes from within the unreal matrix of form. The illusory world of form is governed only by the One Life.

ILLUMINATION 115

Having lost track of our real identity as the eternal One Being that has orchestrated this amazing Creation of individuated forms, we have felt lost and alone. The feeling that there is an over-seeing power that has abandoned us has formed thousands of religious practices.

The ages have seen man, in various forms and stages of self-pity, piety and false humility, bargain with, appease and try to please and control his deities. The self-pity could only be assuaged by holier-than-thou self-importance. Self-pity has been a major obstacle to the discovery that we have begged alms from ourselves.

ILLUMINATION 116

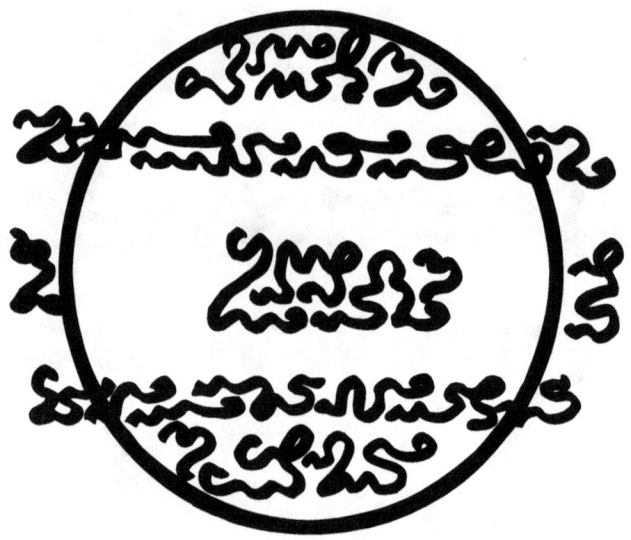

Self-importance has been a less painful illusion than self-pity. We clung to any perceived illusory advantage over others so that we did not have to acknowledge how lost we felt or how unreal the only life we knew was. When we did find the real and holy, we found ourselves in so much vastness that we contracted in angst. The way we could stay in contraction was to enter into more and more doctrine and dogma, often at the point of overzealous bigotry.

The going back and forth in our silent times between the matrix and the formless place of True Beingness until we live from there is our trailblazing answer to this illusional dilemma.

ILLUMINATION 117

There is no real disagreement if we consider that there are no two beings in existence – only One. What then lies behind this seeming friction? It is the opportunity to step out of the unreal.

There are no separate pieces within the One, nor can there be anything inharmonious. When we step out of the unreal we become like anti-matter within matter, cancelling out our own illusion. In this way we thin the veils and the illusory reality becomes a little less pervasive.

ILLUMINATION 118

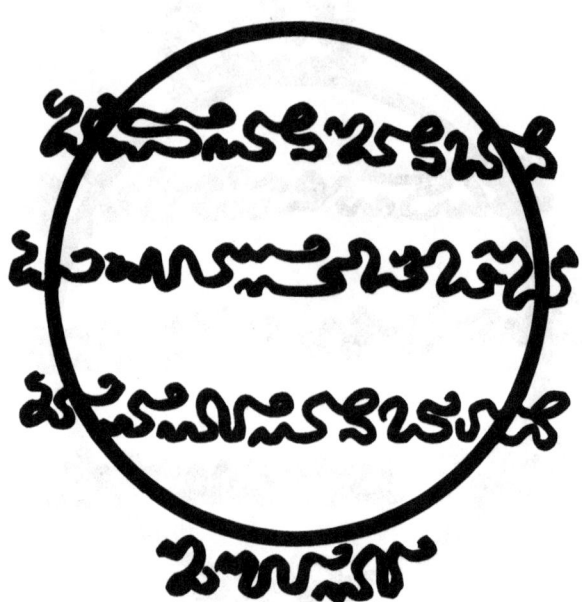

Much control has been exerted to create conformity among those we think should be our 'tribe'. Whether it is within family units, churches or communities, if there is sameness, one is accepted. If not, there is even ostracism or at best a withholding of approval.

The irony is that there is no sameness anywhere at any time. Every snowflake, flower or insect has its own individuality of appearance and expression of the One Life. The quest for sameness is illusory – it doesn't exist.

ILLUMINATION 119

The desires of the tribe, or controlling individuals for the sake of conformity, have created equally illusory tools – appropriateness and propriety.

The self-appointed arbiters of what is 'decent' and 'fitting' and what is not, have a mentor that pervasively spanned all created life – mind. Mind was also a self-appointed magistrate and absolute tyrant. It does not like nonconformity either, since it only feels comfortable with labels and predictability. Anything that challenges its control system is either ignored, attacked or ridiculed. Real Life cannot be lived within the illusion of a tribe.

ILLUMINATION 120

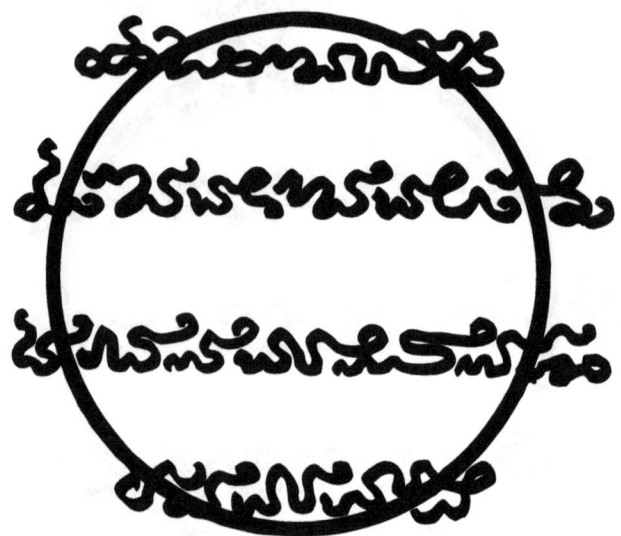

If nothing is out of place, how has an illusion-filled reality found its existence? There is an unreal delight being created like a pearl in an oyster. The timing of its fruition is vital, as is the ability to develop strength and refinement created during its incubation period.

The illusion is both its embryonic sac and its timing mechanism. The illusional membranes will thin, allowing the birth at the correct developmental stage. The illusions within that are being discarded as obsolete are like the potter's clay falling away to reveal a refined creation.

ILLUMINATION 121

We think we are in control of ourselves but in truth, the body's life is so unreal, it is no more than a puppet on a string. Control is a myth, as is being 'out of control'.

At times we feel so expanded it seems we are out of control of our lives. Even expanded, we are still within the One Being who runs our lives. It does not take our direct focus to run our lives.

Those who enter into Immortal Mastery know this principle well, for in this stage of human evolution, speech, writing and living all occur within the total silence of mind.

ILLUMINATION 122

Thinking we are incomplete creates the illusion of achievement as a measuring stick of our worth. There is no achievement when there is no choice.

This matrix is like a dream – not really there. If within a dream the baker bakes good cookies, whose accomplishment is it? Is it the baker's or the dreamer's? It is the same way with our lives. We have come from the deeper levels of the dream into those more shallow. Yet we presume to look back and either cringe at our incompleteness or pat ourselves on the back for our accomplishments. But we have done neither. The Dreamer has been the one orchestrating the dream. The One Life has been pulling the strings.

ILLUMINATION 123

To fear we will encounter a void or a profoundly boring passivity when we enter the One Life is far from the truth. Multiple experiences of the One are required as we exit from the Dream for us to realize that we cannot see It, hear It or encounter It with any of our senses, even the inner ones. It must be experienced in Its boundlessness as we dissolve into It. It is our home, our being, ancient beyond any beginning. Yet we have forgotten how to participate in Our Being.

Realization will come back to us the more we see the realms of life and the more we shed the illusory spiderweb of form that overlays the perfection.

ILLUMINATION 124

Society has been seen as the supporter and creator of order, a surrogate parent to us. It has promised to provide us with amenities we believe we cannot live without in return for our obedience to its laws and rules. The manmade illusional structure of society is not needed to take care of us.

We are governed by the One Life and do not need institutions that promise us comfort, but then put us in bondage through debt and taxes. Our societies have generated enslavement to work and class-based structures. These illusions have become tyrants.

ILLUMINATION 125

The remnants of mind feel comfortable with structure. They thrive on clarity of meaning and labels. We see meaning in art, defining and analyzing it in the name of intellectualism and culture.

It is time to experience the purity of life directly, not through structured filters of analyses. Analysis is only another tool of mind, as is intellect. Life is a direct expression of the intangible, available to us only when we are open, spontaneous and trusting, like perpetual children. The promises of mind to provide us with a pristine world have proven untrustworthy.

ILLUMINATION 126

Eons of cataclysmic Earth changes have created fear that we may in some way be bringing them about. It also makes us feel we have lacked the power to prevent them. The Earth can be affected only by our One Life. At no time can our unreal forms affect the Earth's unreal form. Earth too, has an internal, incorruptible part. Our interconnected, inseparable lives are also indivisibly one with the Earth. She is safe in the care of our Eternal Self.

ILLUMINATION 127

Accessing the shallow areas of life is not better than accessing it deeply. All its parts and levels are equally valid. Even if we have shallow experiential interactions, they can never be shallow if by that term we imply life is only partially accessed. Behind the illusory life of form is the vastness of the majestic All.

Through every seemingly insignificant action, the depths of the Infinite Life speak. Through the windows of our experiences, the One sees Itself with delight.

ILLUMINATION 128

The illusion that wisdom exists implies that the indefinable can be labeled and there are static points in the Infinite's unfolding.

Life of form started in smaller 'boxes' of illusional containment. It is the wisdom of yesterday that got us to this point, by breaking open one box after the other. The insights of obsolete moments of dreaming cannot possibly apply to the present. They brought us to where we are, immediately outliving their usefulness as they broke down the walls.

It is time for us to leave behind our boxes of illusion. We are returning home to the Oneness and no wisdom, with its static viewpoints, can serve us there.

ILLUMINATION 129

The illusion of 'correct' or 'incorrect' implies that anything contrary to the real can exist, that life can be in opposition to itself, that opposites can exist. There can be nothing in existence that is out of place or un-whole or contrary to the Divine Perfection that permeates it all.

So much concern is given to making correct choices. Yet by manipulating our discernment and tastes, the One Life ensures that our choices never falter. They are always correct. We may lie back in the arms of the One Life and relax.

ILLUMINATION 130

What we perceive as obstacles, life turns into symbols of inclusion. The oppositions in our lives were never meant to be anything other than an intricate guidance system. The obstacle that suddenly arises on our path is the loving hand of the One Life directing us to go left or right, were we only to take the time to see. By seeing only the wall, we may not notice that when one door closes, another has just opened.

The worst we can imagine is only a wave of the ocean. We will be carried up and over the wave. We are never alone.

ILLUMINATION 131

Fear exists that when we experience the vastness, we may disassociate from life. The life we detach from is not real. We detach from the unreal without separation.

The truth behind this fear of not being able to run our lives is that we never really could do so, as evidenced by the flaws of manmade reality and the many stresses in our lives.

When our lives are surrendered to the Infinite, the fluid pattern becomes one of unfolding perfection – what it was always meant to be.

ILLUMINATION 132

The illusion of pain, as inflicted by others or by life, is a misrepresentation from our illusory belief systems. For the creation of individuated life for the delight of the One Being, an illusional fracturing that created illusory chambers occurred – much like the splitting of a cell. Those cells have been united as one illusion after another has been seen for what it is.

The pain has been the pain of disconnection from our Real Life of Oneness. This has been seen to be the case but, like the air that is as much inside the box as outside it, there has never really been separation, else this illusory world would not have animated life.

ILLUMINATION 133

The sub-creations of our manmade world do not really exist. The real cannot be created by the unreal. The chair we sit on, the room we sleep in – nothing is actually there. It is just the result of mass hypnosis. The child in his playpen may try and build a bridge with his blocks, but at the end of his playtime all will be removed and packed away.

The blocks we have been playing with are the building blocks of life, but ultimately they are unreal.

ILLUMINATION 134

The mystical kingdoms are the reflections of the nuances of man. As such, they are as unreal as we are. All is being gathered back together.

The 144 Illuminations become one; no illusions have ever existed. The God kingdoms are gathered into one kingdom. The Creation of the One Life will soon be ready to leave its incubator and become part of the nuances of Infinite Life. The mystical kingdoms' realities are getting ready to join with whence they came – the human kingdom.

ILLUMINATION 135

We nurture the illusion that we can teach and advise others, thinking we know what is best for them. Their past is illusory and cannot help determine the newness of the moment.

To heal and save, judges and divides. To acknowledge wholeness is to uplift all life by thinning the illusory veils that bind us. Each soul exists in the perfection of his true Oneness. What can we ever teach anyone? This would only perpetuate the illusion of separation by enacting the illusion of relationship.

ILLUMINATION 136

Although we have fluidly tried to release and move beyond the obsolete memories of a past that does not exist, the damaging footprints of that past still mar the sands of our life with their imprints. This is because imagined creations are not able to change and keep pace as fluidly as the unfolding of Infinite Life.

If we are not created as a separate creation but as an everchanging impression of the unfolding nuances of the One Life, then there are no lasting impressions. This is what we have truly always been. Lasting impressions have never been a reality.

ILLUMINATION 137

The imagined momentary spot called Creation, that formed within the Infinite's boundless unfolding, has taken on a life of its own, even though it is unreal. There is no place where the Infinite is not and Its presence permeates even the illusory portion of Its Being, where this imagined creation took place, thereby enlivening it.

Anything the One Life creates or that is not, is a baser addition that cannot exist. Nothing should ever be created; it would detract from the whole and create space. What then are you and I as the One Life? We are beginningless and real, as impressions of the unfolding nuances of the Infinite.

ILLUMINATION 138

Within the true Beingness we are, there are no polarities, no rest or activity, no beingness and doingness. In desiring to experience interaction with the imagined creation, the four levels of dreaming came into being. The Infinite created a dream body and entered into the dream with Its illusory body in the illusion of relationship.

Within the moment formed by the 'pulse' or 'pop' in the timelessness of Infinite Life, all eons of existence occurred. Like an entire book contained on microfilm in the dot of the letter 'i', all life has occurred within the illusion of the moment. It is impossible for dreaming or sleep to occur. It is not possible for a moment to be created in Infinite Life.

ILLUMINATION 139

The definition of illusion is the desire for the unreal to be real. The tools illusion created to fulfill its desire are fantasy, daydreaming and imagination. These three tools gave rise to the three directions of the above, the below and the within. In turn, the first three stages of linear time and illusory creation began.

The Infinite has no actual movement, but unfolding, alternating impressions. The One Life creates the impressions of form for its delight – not as static shapes, but fluid, boundaryless impressions.

ILLUMINATION 140

The illusory way in which we see events unfold within the illusion-based senses of form creates the impressions of continuity and repetitiveness. The factor of the illusion of the moment contributes to this.

Imagine the Infinite beingness in unfolding fluidity. Imagine that within it a 'pop' happens. The pop has just created a moment, because there was a time it occurred and a time it did not. A moment in a place of no-time is an anomaly; something that does not belong. The result is that, like a rubber ball thrown on the floor, it seems to bounce over and over again. This gives the impression of continuity but in fact it's the same moment repeating. Because you imagined it, it was never really there.

ILLUMINATION 141

There can be no over-focus because there is no reference point. There can be no addiction because the One Life can never abandon Itself. The unreal cannot have influence of any kind in seeming desirable or indispensible or real to the One Life, for it does not exist.

When the first pulse within the Infinite became important as something new or attractive, illusion was seemingly born. Yet none of this is real or has ever existed.

Mind was formed by the hypnotic effect of the unreal and the attraction it had for the One life. Thus, one illusion begat another.

ILLUMINATION 142

A heartbeat, like a single pulse, was imagined within the One Life. But because there is no time, it set that moment apart from the no-time. The effect of having a momentary heartbeat was that it repeated itself over and over, like a record that had gotten stuck. The result was that a heartbeat was born. This was extremely confusing and contradictory. It defined a space where it could be most strongly heard or felt. This area could be defined as a heart. Further out from what now became an illusory reference point, the area that was still affected by the heartbeat became a body.

The illusion that anything new can be created, such as a pulse, implies that there is something the Infinite does not know – an impossibility since there is nothing beyond the One Life.

ILLUMINATION 143

As more attention was given to the heartbeat, it was able to receive more and more and became receptive. Femininity was born as an illusion. The imbalance this created generated a lightning flash. The masculine polarity was formed. The split of masculine and feminine from the androgynous One Life gave duality as an illusion. The heart received an electrical shock that split it into four ventricles. Four spaces were created and the four directions were born.

By never having encountered anything unreal before – because in fact it did not exist – the Infinite assumed everything to be real. Now the illusion of seeking to understand the unreal was formed.

ILLUMINATION 144

The seeming splitting created many illusions: that loss or damage could occur and that something could occur outside the One's control. There were many questions that arose and the act of questioning created density of form as it became more real and solid from focusing on it. The created illusional realities we have been in are the result of the Infinite 'fixing' the fracturing of the heart it had formed. Like a wound that develops thick and hard scar tissue, life became dense where the fracturing had occurred.

The embodiment of the part of the Infinite that was focusing on it was drawn into the scar tissue or dense creations by Its questions and mind became an illusory tool for finding the way out of the web of illusion.

THE EQUATION FOR 144 + 1 = 0

The dissolving of the illusion of anything being created

+

The merging of Creation with its Creator

=

Only Life Incorruptible, fully awoken from the Dream

Bonus Section: The Illuminations of Eternal Life

WHEEL OF 144 ILLUMINATIONS

Closing

May the hearts of man fill with hope; no longer a slave to death shall they be ... long ago's secrets whispered on the wind, shall come to set man free.

The fountain of youth once more shall be found, hidden away within the body it resides. That as in eons of long ago, man again a pure life of longevity may know. The ancients lived long upon the land, but as life was resisted, resources waned. Life spans shortened amongst the children of man.

Remove the boundaries and all resources are yours, as you enter into Oneness with the Eternal Source.

Almine

Other books by Almine

Irash Satva Yoga

Yoga, as a spiritual and physical discipline has been practiced in many variations by masters and novices for countless years and is universally accepted as one of the most effective development tools ever created.
Man's physical form in its original state was meant to be self-purifying, self-regenerating and self-transfiguring. Through pristine living and total surrender, it was possible to open gates in the body that would allow life to permeate and flow through it; indefinitely sustaining it.
In Irash Satva Yoga, received by Almine from the Angelic Kingdom, this ancient methodology is exponentially expanded and enhanced by incorporating the alchemies of sound and frequency.
Using easily mastered postures paired with music from Cosmic Sources created specifically for each, the 144 cardinal gates in the mind and body are opened and cleansed of their dross and debris, allowing the practitioner to tap into the abundance of the One Life.

Published: 2010, 94 pages, soft cover, 6 x 9, ISBN: 978-1-934070-95-6

Shrihat Satva Yoga

The human body is unique in that it is an exact microcosm of the macrocosm of created life. There are 12 points along the right, masculine side of the body and the same number on the left side. These are microcosmic replicas of the macrocosmic cycles of life.
The yoga postures are designed to open and remove the debris from these points – the gates of dreaming. This will occur physically through the postures and the music. Dissolving debris also occurs by way of dreaming (triggered by the breathing and eye movements), releasing past issues that caused the blockages in the points

Published 2010, 108 pages, soft cover, 6 x 9, ISBN: 978-1-934070-15-4

Saradesi Satva Yoga
The Yoga of Eternal Youth

As translated from the ancient texts of Saradesi – The Fountain of Youth. The ancient texts speak of time as movement. They affirm that time and space, movement and stillness, are illusions. To sustain any illusion requires an enormous amount of resources. This depletion of resources causes aging and decay. The illusion of polarity, the impossibility that the One Life can be divided and split is brought to resolution by balancing the opposite poles exactly. Only then can they cancel one another out, revealing an incorruptible reality that lies beyond – the reality of Eternal Youth.

Published 2011, 115 pages, soft cover, 6 x 9, ISBN: 978-1-936926-05-3

Other books by Almine

Belvaspata, Angel Healing, Volume I
The Healing Modality of Miracles

Whether you are a beginner or an experienced master of the miraculous healing modality of Belvaspata, this comprehensive guide is an information rich handbook that will serve as your most valuable tool – a compendium of information for everything you need to know to establish yourself as a practitioner of this miraculous healing modality of the angels. Also included are Kaanish, Braamish Ananu and Song of the Self Belvaspata.

Published: 2011, 394 pages, soft cover, 6 x 9, ISBN: 978-1-936926-34-3

Belvaspata, Angel Healing, Volume 2
Healing through Oneness

Fairy Sound Elixir MP3 included

Whether you are a beginner or an experienced master of the miraculous healing modality of Belvaspata, this comprehensive guide is an information rich handbook that will serve as your most valuable tool – a compendium of information for everything you need to know to establish yourself as a practitioner of this miraculous healing modality of the angels. Belvaspata Volume II includes "The Integrated Use of Fragrance Alchemy," which delivers the method to obtain wellness of the emotional, mental and physical bodies through the combined use of Belvaspata, the alchemy of fragrance and the Atlantean Healing Sigils.

Published: 2012, 467 pages, soft cover, 6 x 9, ISBN: 978-1-936926-40-4

Gift of the Unicorns

Sacred Secrets of Unicorn Magic, 3rd Edition NEW

Where have the Unicorns gone? And, what about mystical winged horses, mermaids, and giants – do they exist? The answers to all of our questions about these fabled creatures can be found in The Gift of the Unicorns.

This magical book tells the story of the Unicorns and Pegasus, and their heroism in preserving purity and innocence during the ages of darkness on Earth. In their own words, these beings reveal where they went, the purpose of their golden shoes and the sacred mission they undertook for the Mother of All Creation. What's more, they share long-held secrets about the Earth.

Published: 2012, 188 pages, soft cover, 6 x 9, ISBN: 978-1-936926-48-0

Other books by Almine

Journey to the Heart of God
Second Edition
Mystical Keys to Immortal Mastery

Ground-breaking cosmology revealed for the first time, sheds new light on previous bodies of information such as the Torah, the I Ching and the Mayan Zolkien. The explanation of man's relationship as the microcosm as set out in the previous book A Life of Miracles, is expanded in a way never before addressed by New Age authors, giving new meaning and purpose to human life. Endorsed by an Astro-physicist from Cambridge University and a former NASA scientist, this book is foundational for readers at all levels of spiritual growth.

Published: 2009, 276 pages, soft cover, 6 x 9, ISBN: 978-1-934070-26-0

Secrets Of The Hidden Realms
Third Edition
Mystical Keys to the Unseen Worlds

This remarkable book delves into mysteries few mystics have ever revealed. It gives in detail:
- The practical application of the Goddess mysteries
- Secrets of the angelic realms
- The maps, alphabets, numerical systems of Lemuria, Atlantis, and the Inner Earth
- The Atlantean calender, accurate within 5 minutes
- The alphabet of the Akashic libraries.

Secrets of the Hidden Realms amazing bridge across the chasm that has separated humanity for eons from unseen realms.

Published: 2011, 412 pages, soft cover, 6 x 9, ISBN: 978-1-936926-38-1

The Ring of Truth
Third Edition
Sacred Secrets of the Goddess

As man slumbers in awareness, the nature of his reality has altered forever. As one of the most profound mystics of all time, Almine explains this dramatic shift in cosmic laws that is changing life on earth irrevocably. A powerful healing modality is presented to compensate for the changes in the laws regarding energy that healers have traditionally relied upon. The new principles of beneficial white magic and the massive changes in spiritual warriorship are meticulously explained.

Published: 2009, 260 pages, soft cover, 6 x 9, ISBN: 978-1-934070-28-4

Other books by Almine

Handbook for Healers
The Healing Wisdom of the Seer Almine

Handbook for Healers is an invaluable tool for anyone interested in self-healing or the healing of others. It offers both practical and spiritual guidance gleaned from the globally acclaimed Seer Almine's advice to her students during the past decade. It reveals vital information on rejuvenating the body and understanding its communication through the language of pain, and many more empowering insights.

Published: 2013, 648 pages, soft cover, 6 x 9, ISBN: 978-1-936926-44-2

Visit Almine's website www.spiritualjourneys.com for world-wide retreat locations and dates, online courses, radio shows and more. Order one of Almine's many books, CDs or an instant download. US toll-free phone: 1-877-552-5646

Music by Almine

Children of the Sun

Music from the Known Planets (Re-mastered and re-titled version of the Interstellar Sound Elixirs)

The beautiful interstellar sound elixirs received and sung by Almine.

Price $9.95 MP3 Download
$14.95 CD

Labyrinth of the Moon

Music from the Hidden Planets (Re-titled version of the Sound Elixirs of the Hidden Planets)

All the vocals in these elixirs are received and sung in the moment by Almine

Price $9.95 MP3 Download
$14.95 CD

Jubilation - Songs of Praise

Music from around the world to lift the heart and inspire the listener.

The extraordinary mystical quality of the music, and the exquisite clarity of Almine's voice, creates the ambient impression of being in the presence of angels.

Price $9.95 MP3 Download
$14.95 CD

www.ingramcontent.com/pod-product-compliance
Lightning Source LLC
Chambersburg PA
CBHW060449170426
43199CB00011B/1146